Dr Onyója Momoh is a recognised expert in the field of international family law, specialising in cross-border children proceedings. She was called to the Bar in 2010 (*Gray's Inn*) and is consistently ranked as a leading barrister in the Legal 500 UK for children law since 2017. Onyója undertook her LLM, Ph.D., and post-doctoral research (EU-funded POAM project) all in the area of international parental child abduction and the protection of children across international frontiers. Alongside practice, she teaches private international law (family law) at the University of Aberdeen and has published book chapters, peer-reviewed journal articles, prepared country and expert reports, as well as delivered training and lectures around the world.

In recent years, Onyója has engaged in high level advisory and advocacy activities within Government ministries (with a particular interest in Nigeria, and sub-Saharan Africa), the judiciary, and charities abroad, as well as an invited expert presenting at forums such as the Hague Conference on Private International Law, the European Commission and the UK House of Lords Justice and Home Affairs Committee.

A Practical Guide to International Parental Child Abduction Law (England and Wales)

A Practical Guide to International Parental Child Abduction Law (England and Wales)

Onyója Momoh, BA (Hons)., LL.M., Ph.D.

Barrister, (Eng. & Wales), Gray's Inn

Lecturer in Private International Law, University of Aberdeen

Law Brief Publishing

Published 2023 by Law Brief Publishing, an imprint of Law Brief Publishing Ltd
30 The Parks
Minehead
Somerset
TA24 8BT

www.lawbriefpublishing.com

Paperback: 978-1-914608-79-7

This book is dedicated to the main protagonists in every case: the children. To their journeys, whatever the story might be.

FOREWORD

I met Onyója on my first visit to Aberdeen University and noted her talent. She has the advantage of being at the same time both an academic and a practicing member of the Bar. That gives her a balanced perspective broader than she would have were she just an academic or just a practicing barrister. That strength is manifest from this succinct guide. Busy lawyers want a guide that is above all practical and not overburdened by too much analysis of lofty authorities. The 1980 Hague Convention is essentially a procedural tool to achieve the return of the abducted child to the jurisdiction of habitual residence. Arguably States party to the Convention have been guilty of lapsing too readily into an improper review of welfare issues. Arguably the most distinguished judges have been tempted to theorise too much in what should be a straightforward domain. This handbook avoids such pitfalls and rightly focuses on what the generalist family lawyer should do when confronted with a Convention case. I do not doubt that it has a useful place on many a lawyer's bookshelf.

The Rt. Hon. Sir Mathew Thorpe
Former Lord Justice of Appeal (England and Wales),
Inaugural Head of International Family Justice for England
and Wales and Vice-President of the Family Division
July 2023

PREFACE

We have settled into an England without EU laws, but it is no underestimation of the many important and influential decisions on international child abduction from this jurisdiction. Whereas this book is not intended to explore the substantial case law in this area, the objective is to enable practitioners to acquire or refine competence in navigating this field of international private law. It will also steer readers towards sources for wider reading and deeper understanding. Far from simply engaging in a formulaic approach to child abduction cases, it is hoped that the book offers practitioners the confidence to examine issues that truly matter for their client. As such, the penultimate chapter in this book reflects on certain topics such as child participation, migrant parents, the approach to allegations of domestic abuse, and access to legal aid.

With a deep appreciation for the many legal scholars, judges, practitioners, and other experts who continue to respond to the challenges in this area; past, present and future, I also warmly acknowledge colleagues in my own journey, in both academia and practice. I have learnt a great deal from their abundance of knowledge and experience, generously shared. Finally, my gratitude would not be complete without thanking my family, friends, and God.

I have aimed to state the law as reflected in the sources available to me on 1st June 2023.

Onyója Momoh
June 2023

CONTENTS

CHAPTER ONE

INTRODUCTION

Epictetus tells us that 'if your choices are beautiful, so too will you be'. However, in the complexities of international parental child abduction, mobilizing choices that are far from beautiful is commonplace. Even so, surely, these actions can in some instances be separated from the nature of their makers. A phenomenon of its time, when back in the late 1970s, legal kidnapping was the term used to describe parental child abduction. Perspectives had to shift from the idea that abduction could only be a criminal act to the notion that parents could abduct their children; recognising the harmful and potentially irremediable consequences[1] for the child. Harm which is compounded by the passage of time especially within a child's sense of time. When a child is removed (e.g., covertly) or retained away (e.g., following a holiday abroad) from their country of habitual residence, against the custody rights of another with parental responsibility or without court permission (for example, a relocation order), parental child abduction occurs. When child abduction is alleged, it is necessary that legal practitioners are quickly adept on foremost aspects: jurisdiction, applicable law, recognition, and enforcement. While emulating the rules of private international law, from an ordinary perspective of legal practitioner to client, when presented with a set of facts, it is as adequate a *modus operandi* as any. You ask yourself, *where* has the child been removed to or from; which court is seised? Does a multilateral or bilateral treaty apply or does one turn to our national laws; with a return order often being the desired outcome, how might that be

---

[1]   Professor Marilyn Freeman, 'International Child Abduction: Is It All Back to Normal Once the Child Returns Home?' (2011) International Family Law, 39-51: effects on children including physical symptoms of stress, non-physical effects (lack of faith, feeling helplessness), guilt towards one or both parents, lack of trust, extremely bad behaviour, hostility, general insecurity, sibling jealousy.

recognised and enforced? These key questions often reflect the distinction between whether one utilises international instruments or national laws.

The jurisdictional framework for international child abduction cases should be the starting point, it sets apart 'Convention' and 'Non-Convention' cases. Forging the bridge between legal systems and legal rules, the main and perhaps most familiar treaty is the *1980 Hague Convention on the Civil Aspects of International Child Abduction* ('the Convention', 'the 1980 Hague Convention') and it is on this premise that the term 'Convention' or 'non-Convention' flows. It is hoped that this book will serve as a practical guide and springboard for barristers, solicitors and other stakeholders in this field, whether experienced or novice. Recalling the words of Holman J in *Re H (child abduction; wrongful retention)* [2000] 3 FCR 412 where professionals involved in children cases, judges, and practitioners were reminded that: –

> *'Although child abduction is a specialist branch of family law, anyone involved in children cases must be alert to the possibility of international child abduction whenever a child has formerly lived abroad in a Convention country and a parent wishes to return to that country with him. The concept and ambit of 'wrongful retention'² extends the arm of the Hague Convention well beyond a 'snatch' and means that it can apply after a child has been in the jurisdiction for a substantial period of time. Alarm bells should ring at once, and if there is any doubt at all consideration should be given to transferring the case to a full-time judge of the Family Division and/or to seeking expert advice of the Child Abduction Unit. Moreover, if a solicitor, though acting for the 'abducting' parent, appreciates even the possibility that the Hague Convention might apply, he is under an important duty to draw that fact to the attention of the court at the first opportunity in any legal proceedings.'*

To set the parameters, the book is concerned with international child abduction outside the UK. Abductions between say England and

Scotland are not international abductions so to speak and the way the law currently stands, the 1980 Hague Convention would not apply. Note also that whereas the 'court' or 'English court' is used interchangeably, it regards the jurisdiction of both England and Wales. This book will focus on international child abduction to England and Wales, often referred to as *incoming* cases, as this is the main perspective that practitioners will deal with. Lest we forget, however, that when children are abducted *out of* England and Wales from a Convention or non-Convention State – *outgoing cases* – practitioners will need to be cognizant of the distinction between available remedies and instances where international abductions will engage our domestic courts as opposed to, or in addition to the foreign court. These aspects will also be explored. Whilst there will be an understandable absence of previously relevant EU instruments in this book, in particular Brussels IIa[2] (now Brussels IIter)[3], the 1980 Hague Convention and its interactions with the 1996 Hague Convention[4] will gain focus, shored up by the 2010 Family Procedural Rules, Part 12, Chapter 6; Practice Directions 12J, 12D and 12F; as well as the updated 2023 President's Guide on Case Management and Mediation of International Child Abduction Proceedings.

---

[2] Council Regulation (EC) No 2201/2003 of 27 November 2003 concerning jurisdiction and the recognition and enforcement of judgments in matrimonial matters and the matters of parental responsibility, repealing Regulation (EC) No 1347/2000.

[3] Council Regulation (EU) 2019/1111 of 25 June 2019 on jurisdiction, the recognition and enforcement of decisions in matrimonial matters and the matters of parental responsibility, and on international child abduction (hereafter: 'Brussels IIter', 'the Recast Regulation').

[4] 1996 Hague Convention on Jurisdiction, Applicable Law, Recognition, Enforcement and Co-operation in Respect of Parental Responsibility and Measures for the Protection of Children (hereafter: 'the 1996 Hague Child Protection', 'the 1996 Convention').

CHAPTER TWO

CHILD ABDUCTIONS TO AND FROM ENGLAND AND WALES

Firstly, a distinction should be drawn between child abductions into and out of England and Wales, also referred to as *incoming* and *outgoing* cases respectively. This will be the difference between knowing when to issue an application in the English High Court or the foreign court where the child has been taken to. In the latter scenario, English lawyers would need to be prepared to advice and where necessary, assist the client with contacting the International Child Abduction and Contact Unit for England and Wales ('ICACU'), who will in turn set in motion access to a suitable legal representative in the foreign Hague State that the child has been taken to. ICACU is the Central Authority for the operation of the 1980 Hague Convention. In essence, an outgoing case will concern the abduction of a child from England and Wales to another jurisdiction. Whereas incoming applications concern cases with a child being abducted to England and Wales, and most applications from the 'left behind' parent, if not all, will come via ICACU. Where the Hague Convention is concerned, in both instances, incoming cases are dealt with in the English courts, all cases are lodged in and will commence in London and will be heard at the High Court of the Family Division. The High Court has exclusive jurisdiction in such cases (Child Abduction and Custody Act 1985, section 4), with the concentration of jurisdiction being an obvious advantage. In a Hague outgoing case, the foreign court to which the child has been removed to or retained would hear the application for the summary return of the child to England and Wales.

An application under the court's inherent jurisdiction in respect of non-Convention cases is made under Form C66, whereas a Hague Convention application is made under Form C67.

In addition to ICACU, the community of international child abduction specialists also involves the Office of the Head of International Family Justice.[5] The office liaises with members of the International Hague Network of Judges[6] and the European Judicial Network of Judges, addressing enquiries on international family law cases. The inaugural head The Rt. Hon. Sir Mathew Thorpe LJ is superseded by the current Head, Lord Justice Moylan, and Deputy Head, Mr Justice MacDonald.[7] The Office is crucial, not only in its role in assisting and training judges in this jurisdiction and abroad, but also in contributing to the development of family law, practice, and policy.

Further, from a public access perspective, Reunite is a charity specialised in offering advice, assistance, and mediation to the public on international parental child abduction. Reunite is also engaged in research and policy, and frequently intervenes in proceedings. The charity is part funded by the UK Ministry of Justice and UK Foreign and Commonwealth Office.[8]

---

[5] https://www.judiciary.uk/about-the-judiciary/international/international-family-justice/. The office may be contacted by email at IFJOffice@Justice.gov.uk or by telephone: +44 (0) 2079477197, as of 20 June 2023.

[6] See https://www.hcch.net/en/instruments/conventions/specialised-sections/child-abduction/ihnj.

[7] Also the International Hague Network Judges for England and Wales.

[8] Reunite International Child Abduction Centre, PO Box 7124, Leicester LE1 7XX United Kingdom. Telephone number: +44(0)116 255 6234, Email: adviceline@reunite.org, Internet: www.reunite.org.

2.1 Child Abduction to England and Wales

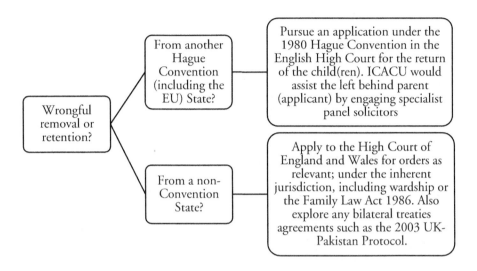

2.2 Child Abduction from England and Wales

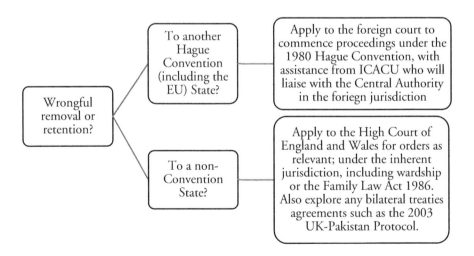

2.3 When Should You Apply to the English High Court?

An application may be made to the High Court for the return of a child(ren) who has been abducted from a Hague Convention State where s/he was habitually resident prior to the removal to or retention in England and Wales. Practitioners are encouraged to familiarise themselves with relevant provisions under Practice Direction 12F – International Child Abduction as well as the Family Procedural Rules 2010.

An application may also be brought under the inherent jurisdiction of the High Court for the return of a child(ren) who has been abducted from England and Wales to a non-Convention State, or vice versa. On the former scenario, habitual residence is mostly the jurisdictional basis, and this is explored further in chapter 4.1. However, see also below other arguments that may be advanced. Practitioners are encouraged to familiarise themselves with relevant provisions under Practice Direction 12D – Inherent Jurisdiction (including Wardship Proceedings) and FPR 2010. Note however, that there are also other important criteria before an application can be successfully issued, and this is explored further in subsequent chapters.

Where an outgoing case ends up in the English court and, say, an application under section 8 of the Children Act 1989 is brought in tandem with or in advance of a 1980 Hague application in the foreign court, there must be good reason as to why the court should depart from the proper and effective mechanism available to Hague Convention countries (see (S (Abduction – Hague Convention or BIIa) [2018] EWCA Civ 1226 [47]). Absence good reason, such as a potentially persuasive argument for declaratory relief e.g., a declaration of habitual residence, as per (S (Abduction – Hague Convention or BIIa) the 'better course for the court is to defer making a return order until an application under the 1980 Hague Convention has been determined in the other Member State.' Though this related to Brussels IIa, the same argument persists in relation to a different course of remedy other than the 1980 Hague

Convention if available, including the 1996 Hague Convention. To pursue applications notwithstanding the aforementioned runs the risk of criticisms, delays, expense, and in essence, a scatter gun approach that may well be ineffectual.

2.4 Other Jurisdictional Arguments

2.4.1 Forum Conveniens

Briefly on this topic, in a non-Convention case, an application under the inherent jurisdiction of the High Court may raise jurisdictional arguments. This may be on the basis that the English Court has jurisdiction but so does the other country, e.g., because it is the country first seised on account of extant proceedings or because it is asserted that habitual residence can be established in that country. In these circumstances, a question arises on the issue of the appropriate forum for the case to be heard. At this juncture, it is helpful for practitioners to refer to the guidance provided by MacDonald J in *W v F (Forum Conveniens)* [2019] EWHC 1995 (Fam) at para 30:

> 30. Where the English court does have jurisdiction under Art 8 but there are proceedings also in a third-party non-member state the issue becomes one of *forum conveniens*. As I have already noted, the issue of *forum conveniens* is to be determined by reference to the principles set out in the case of *Spiliada Maritime Corporation v Consulex* [1997] AC 460. These cardinal principles can be stated as follows:
>
> i) It is upon the party seeking a stay of the English proceedings to establish that it is appropriate;
>
> ii) A stay will only be granted where the court is satisfied that there is some other forum available where the case may be more suitably tried for the interests of all parties and the ends

of justice. Thus, the party seeking a stay must show not only that England is not the natural and appropriate forum but that there is another available forum that is clearly and distinctly more appropriate;

iii) The court must first consider what is the 'natural forum', namely that place with which the case has the most real and substantial connection. Connecting factors will include not only matters of convenience and expense but also factors such as the relevant law governing the proceedings and the places where the parties reside;

iv) If the court concludes having regard to the foregoing matters that another forum is more suitable than England it should normally grant a stay unless the other party can show that there are circumstances by reason of which justice requires that a stay should nevertheless be refused. In determining this, the court will consider all the circumstances of the case, including those which go beyond those taken into account when considering connecting factors.

31. In determining the appropriate forum in cases concerning children using the principles in *Spiliada Maritime Corporation v Consulex*, the child's best interests would not appear to be paramount, but rather an important consideration (whilst in *H v H (Minors)(Forum Conveniens)(Nos 1 and 2)* [1993] 1 FLR 958 at 972 Waite J (as he then was) held that the child's interests were paramount, subsequent decisions have treated those interests as an important consideration: *Re S (Residence Order: Forum Conveniens)* [1995] 1 FLR 314 at 325, *Re V (Forum Conveniens)* [2005] 1 FLR 718 and *Re K* [2015] EWCA Civ 352).

32. The starting point when determining whether the party seeking the stay has established that England is not the appropriate forum for a case concerning a child is that the court with the pre-eminent claim to jurisdiction is the place where the child habitually resides (although habitual residence will not be a conclusive factor). In *Re M (Jurisdiction: Forum Conveniens)* [1995] 2 FLR 224 at 225G Waite LJ observed as follows:

> "There is no limit, in legal theory, to the jurisdiction of the court in England to act in the interests of any child who happens to be within the jurisdiction for whatever purpose and for however short a time. In practice, however, if the child is not habitually resident in this country and there are legal procedures in the country of habitual residence available to achieve a fair hearing of competing parental claims regarding the child's upbringing, the English court will decline jurisdiction, except for the purpose of making whatever orders are necessary to ensure a speedy and peaceful return of the child to the country of habitual residence. The practice thus is to follow the spirit of the Convention, even though its formal terms are inapplicable."

2.4.2 Nationality

In relation to nationality, the Supreme Court case of *Re B (A Child)* [2016] UKSC 4 rejected the argument that the nationality-based jurisdiction falls for exercise only in cases 'at the extreme end of the spectrum,' the dicta, as per Lady Hale, and Lord Toulson, provides at para. 60 that '...the basis of the jurisdiction, as was pointed out by Pearson LJ in *In re P (GE) (An Infant)* [1965] Ch 568, at 587, is that 'an infant of British nationality, whether he is in or outside this country, owes a duty of allegiance to the Sovereign and so is entitled to protection.'

The real question is whether the circumstances are such that this British child requires that protection. For our part we do not consider that the inherent jurisdiction is to be confined by a classification which limits its exercise to 'cases which are at the extreme end of the spectrum', per McFarlane LJ in *In re N (Abduction: Appeal)* [2012] EWCA Civ 1086; [2013] 1 FLR 457, para 29.' With this in mind, evoking jurisdiction on the basis of nationality, especially where tensions exist in relation to the concept of comity, should implore the need for protection and be approached with circumspection.

CHAPTER THREE

THE OPERATION OF
THE 1980 HAGUE
CONVENTION

3.1 The Hague Conference on Private International Law

Before exploring the 1980 Hague Convention, it is worth understanding the force behind it. The Hague Conference on Private International Law ('HCCH', 'the Hague Conference') is a global inter-governmental organization which became a permanent international institution with the entry into force of its Statute in 1955.[9] The activities of the Hague Conference are coordinated by a multinational Secretariat known as the Permanent Bureau. The organization is principally governed and funded by its members and over the years it has become renowned as a Centre for international judicial and administrative co-operation in the area of private law, particularly in the fields of family and children, of civil procedure and commercial law.[10] From the outset, the work of the Hague Conference has been championed, with founding participating experts being described as 'serious men[11]...going to The Hague on the greatest mission on which any of them ever left their countries...',[12] in

---

[9]   Statue of the Hague Conference on Private International Law (adopted on 21 October 1951, entered into force on 15 July 1955).

[10] Https://www.hcch.net/en/about, accessed 1 June 2023.

[11] And women as our current times amply demonstrate.

[12] Hague Conference on Private International Law, 'The Advocate of Peace' (1907) 69(6) Work Affairs Institute, 125.

anticipation of working with an organisation destined for 'great success'[13] and that 'cannot fail'.[14]

Article 1 of the Statute provides that the Hague Conference's purpose is to work for the 'progressive unification of the rules of private international law'[15] and by doing so finding internationally agreed approaches. The Hague Conference meets to negotiate and adopt Conventions and to decide upon future work with the aim of finding solutions to problems arising in the realms of private international law. The Council on General Affairs and Policy, which comprises of all Members of the Hague Conference, meets every year to discuss proposals on the agenda whilst operating through a Permanent Bureau.[16] The Permanent Bureau, which has its seat at The Hague,[17] is in charge of the preparation and organisation of the Hague Conference sessions and meetings of the Council and Special Commissions.[18] Special Commissions are set up by the Council to prepare draft Conventions or review issues on private international law pertinent to the work of the Hague Conference.[19]

---

[13] ibid.

[14] ibid.

Article 1, Statue of the Hague Conference on Private International Law. See also generally Georges A. L. Droz, 'A Comment on the Role of the Hague Conference on Private International Law' (1994) 57(3) Law and Contemporary Problems 8, 3: the session's fourth commission comments on the role of the Hague Conference being 'a great part of private international law'.

[16] Statue of the Hague Conference on Private International Law, Article 4.

[17] ibid Article 5.

[18] ibid Article 6.

[19] ibid Article 8.

On 24 October 1980, the Hague Conference adopted the 1980 Hague Convention.[20] Since this day, the Convention's practical operation has been regularly reviewed by Special Commissions.[21] The 1980 Hague Convention is regarded for is successes[22] and has been described as 'perhaps the best-known treaty emanating from the Hague Conference, and world-wide is the best known of the various arrangements regulating the cross-border movement of children'.[23]

The Special Commissions of the Hague Conference are regarded as a team of national experts who are designated with the task of reviewing the operation of the Conventions and adopting recommendations.[24] The objective is to enable improvements in the effectiveness of the Conventions and 'to promote consistent practices and interpretation'.[25] It also aims to support the cooperation among Contracting States in the implementation of Conventions.[26] During the period from 23rd to 26th

---

[20] The Hague Convention: Status table as of 1 June 2023; there are 103 Contracting States to the Hague Convention.

[21] E.g., see generally Permanent Bureau of the Hague Conference Summaries of Part I and II: 'Conclusions and Recommendations adopted by the Sixth Meeting of the Special Commission on the Practical Operation of the 1980 and 1996 Hague Conventions' (Part I – June 2011).

[22] See Paul Beaumont and Peter McEleavy, *The Hague Convention on International Child Abduction* (Oxford University Press, Oxford 1999) 4 and 23-27: the successes of the Hague Convention are also attributed to the strengths and successes of the Hague model.

[23] Duncan Ranton, 'Hague and Non-Hague Convention Abductions: Notes for Reunite Website on Hague Convention Law' (20 October 2009) 2.

[24] Https://www.hcch.net/en/about, accessed 1 June 2023

[25] ibid.

[26] Carol S Bruch and Margaret Durkin, 'The Hague's Online Child Abduction Materials: A Trap for the Unwary' (2010) 44(1) Family Law Quarterly, 68-69 citing A Dyer, 'Report on International Child Abduction by One Parent Legal Kidnapping', Preliminary Document No 1 of August 1978, III Hague Conference On Private International Law, Actes et Documents of the XIVth Session (Child Abduction) (1980) 20.

October 1989, a Special Commission meeting[27] was held to review the practical operation of the 1980 Hague Convention. After the first Special Commission meeting, it was agreed that periodic meetings on the operation of the 1980 Hague Convention would be particularly useful. It was intended that such meetings could improve the co-operation and effectiveness of Central Authorities and help to ensure the appropriate operation and implementation of the Convention.[28] The 1989 Special Commission meeting was convened by the Secretary General and was attended by thirty States and seven NGOs. The meeting was intended for Member States of the Hague Conference, whether or not they were party to the 1980 Hague Convention and other intergovernmental and non-governmental international organizations with an interest in the treaty.[29] Seven Special Commissions later and with an eight imminently on the way, the review of the operation of the treaties now combine the 1980 Hague Convention and 1996 Hague Convention. Where the 1980 Hague Convention is concerned, it is supported, amongst others, by the Guide to Good Practice Part I – Central Authority Practice 2003, the Guide to Good Practice Part II – Implementing Measures 2003, the Guide to Good Practice Part III – Preventive Measures 2005, the Guide to Good Practice Part IV – Enforcement 2010, the Guide to Good Practice Part V – Mediation 2012, and the Guide to Good Practice Part VI – Article 13(1)(b) 2020. Practitioners are invited to familiarise themselves with these.

Other useful sources include INCADAT, the International Child Abduction database which contains and enables the search of child

---

[27] Thirty countries were represented at the first meeting of the Special Commission, ten of which were then Parties, while two IGOs and seven INGOs were represented by observers.

[28] Permanent Bureau of the Hague Conference, 'Overall Conclusions of the Special Commission of October 1989 on the Operation of the Hague Convention of 25 October 1980 on the Civil Aspects of International Child Abduction' (1989) paras. 16 and 62.

[29] ibid, para. 2.

abduction case law, including summaries and analyses, references to house publications such as Guides to Good Practice and the Judges' Newsletter.[30] It is run by an editorial team headed by Professor Peter McEleavy.

INCASTAT[31] is the International Child Abduction Statistical Database launched on 28 September 2007 to encourage the maintenance of accurate statistics concerning cases dealt with by Central Authorities under the 1980 Hague Convention. See also Report on the iChild Pilot and the Development of the International Child Abduction Statistical Database, INCASTAT (2006)[32] and subsequent review of its operation.[33]

Finally, IHNJ is the International Hague Network of Judges. A network campaigned for by Lord Justice Thorpe, one of its founding members. To this day, judicial communication and cooperation is championed through IHNJ. With a fundamental purpose of developing inter-State cooperation at judicial level, the network aims to foster the exchange of practice and information with designated judges in Contracting States who are often the first port of call. In addition to promoting mutual understanding and thus consistency in the implementation of the 1980 Hague Convention, on a practical level, an example is the useful benefit of liaison amongst judicial authorities to ensure the validity and adequacy

---

[30] The Judges' Newsletter on International Child Protection on the HCCH website at https://www.hcch.net/en/instruments/conventions/publications2/judges-newsletter.

[31] See 'INCADAT explained' at https://www.incadat.com/en, accessed 20 May 2023. See also INCADAT Guide for Correspondents.

[32] See HCCH Report on the iChild Pilot, http://www.hcch.net/upload/wop/abd_pd09e2006.pdf, accessed 20 May 2023.

[33] HCCH 'Status and use of INCASTAT – a Critical Assessment', Preliminary Document No. 7, CGAP 2021, https://assets.hcch.net/docs/d2a079c2-167b-481f-8d56-e2881447ab4a.pdf, accessed 20 May 2023. Recent reviews of its effectiveness and consideration of reform to improve the collection of data and to ensure a more effect tool.

of conditions and protective measures attached to return orders. The designated IHNJ for England and Wales also occupy the office of the IFJ: Lord Justice Moylan and Mr Justice MacDonald.[34]

3.2 The Objectives of the Convention

The 1980 Hague Convention has been readily implemented in England and Wales since 1986, tackling what was then viewed as an emergent issue of international child abduction. The key word from this well-known multilateral treaty is the 'civil'[35] aspects of international abduction, as is the focus of this book from a family law perspective. The Convention was domesticated in England and Wales pursuant to the Child Abduction and Custody Act 1985. It has grown to 103 Contracting States[36] and counting. Of importance is noting that cases can only be dealt with under the 1980 Hague Convention if it is in force between the States concerned. Thus, having two contracting States does not necessarily mean that the Convention will apply. See for example, the position with regards to the United Kingdom[37] and Pakistan. The United Kingdom has not accepted Pakistan's accession as yet; therefore,

---

[34] HCCH Members of the International Hague Network of Judges (June 2023) https://assets.hcch.net/docs/665b2d56-6236-4125-9352-c22bb65bc375.pdf.

[35] Note nevertheless, that pursuant to section 1 of the Child Abduction Act 1984, a criminal offence is committed when 'a person connected with a child under the age of sixteen…takes or sends the child out of the United Kingdom without the appropriate consent', namely anyone with parental responsibility for the child. It is also a criminal offence a person unconnected with the child to act in the similar manner.

[36] Https://www.hcch.net/en/instruments/conventions/status-table/?cid=24, accessed June 2023.

[37] The United Kingdom, as opposed to England and Wales, on the basis that the Convention was ratified by the UK. Note, however, the operational distinction between cases to England and Wales, Scotland, or Northern Ireland.

the Convention does not operate bilaterally between the UK (say for example as the *requested State* – the country the child was removed to) and Pakistan (the *requesting State* – the country the child was taken from). If a case ensued between England and Pakistan, it would be regarded as a non-Convention case.

The preamble to the Convention is abundantly clear of its aims:

> 'Firmly convinced that the interests of children are of paramount importance in matters relating to their custody…desiring to protect children internationally from the harmful effects of their wrongful removal or retention…as well as to secure protection for rights of access.'

The Convention's objective is to ensure that children who have been wrongfully removed or retained away from the country of their habitual residence, in breach of the rights of custody of another parent (or other person, institution or body with parental responsibility), are returned immediately. Article 12(1) provides that a return shall be ordered forthwith. In *Re D (A Child) (Abduction: Rights of Custody)* [2006] UKHL 51; [2007] 1 FLR 961 Baroness Hale states that:

> 'The whole object of the convention is to secure the swift return of children wrongfully removed from their home country, not only so that they can return to the place which is properly their "home", but also so that any dispute about where they should live in the future can be decided in the courts of their home country, according to the laws of their home country and in accordance with the evidence which will mostly be there rather than in the country to which they have been removed…'

Mostyn J in *FE v YE* [2017] EWHC 2165 (Fam), [2018] 2 WLR 200 [14] summarises it as follows:

'The nature of the relief which is granted under the 1980 Convention is essentially of an interim, procedural nature. It does no more than to return the child to the home country for the courts of that country to determine his or her long-term future. [...] 15. It is for this reason that the procedure for a claim under the 1980 Convention is summary. Oral evidence is very much the exception rather than the rule. The available defences must be judged strictly in the context of the objective of the limited relief that is sought. Controversial issues of fact need not be decided.'

In summary, the Convention seeks to re-establish a situation unilaterally and forcibly altered by the 'taking' parent. The underlying philosophy is that a child abducted across borders must be promptly returned to their State of habitual residence for substantive welfare decisions to be made by a competent court in that State. Further, it acts as a deterrence for parents who resort to unlawful removals or retention in order to establish artificial jurisdictional links with the State that the child has been removed to or retained in.

The Convention applies to any child 'who was habitually resident in a contracting state immediately before any breach of custody or access rights, therefore ceasing to apply when the child attains the age of 16 years when the application is heard even though the abduction occurred when the child was 15'.[38] In the Convention's Explanatory Report, Professor Elisa Perez-Vera[39] explains that the 1980 Hague Convention seeks to transpose the principle of the interests and welfare of children being paramount to respond to the problem of international child abductions as a whole. Indeed, case law in the late 80's and 90's suggested that the objective of the Hague Convention was to safeguard the interests

---

[38] Article 4, 1980 Hague Convention.

[39] Elisa Perez-Vera, Explanatory Report on the 1980 Hague Child Abduction Convention, Acts and Documents of the Fourteenth Session (1980), 3 Child Abduction 426-476, 431, para. 24 (thereafter 'Perez-Vera Report').

of children collectively rather than individually, but practitioners should not be misled by this; affording each individual child careful consideration must prevail. Professor Perez-Vera makes the point at paragraph 24 that 'the struggle against the great increase in international child abductions must always be inspired by the desire to protect children and should be based upon an interpretation of their true interests...children must no longer be regarded as parents' property, but must be recognized as individuals with their own rights and needs'.[40]

In at least the last two decades, statistics have revealed an important change in the pattern of abduction or rather the perceived abductor. In particular, in contrast to abductions being committed by a noncustodial father, the majority of abductions were being carried out by mothers, usually the primary carer of the child[ren]. In turn, there lies a correlation with the frequency of the Article 13(1)*b)* exception being raised. Even so, one may argue that the rigidity of the 1980 Hague Convention is purposely designed so as to protect the potentially undermining impact that the exceptions to the rule may pose. The 1980 Hague Convention provides uniform laws Contracting States may adopt to compel the return of a child wrongfully removed, 'firmly convinced' that the paramount interests of children lies in their prompt return to the State of habitual residence. It is for the Court to consider the claim that the child was unlawfully removed without successful reliance on an 'exception' and not to consider the merits of an underlying custody claim. Nevertheless, these exceptions are Article 12, Article 13(1)a), Article 13(1)*b)*, Article 13(2) and Article 20 of the Convention.

---

[40] Perez-Vera Report, para. 24, p. 431.

3.3 The Central Authority of England and Wales

The International Child Abduction and Contact Unit (ICACU) is the Central Authority for England and Wales:[41]

The International Child Abduction and Contact Unit (ICACU)

Office of the Official Solicitor & Public Trustee

Post Point 0.53

102 Petty France

London SW1H 9AJ

DX: Post Point 0.53 Official Solicitor & Public Trustee DX 152384

Westminster 8

United Kingdom

Telephone number: tel.: +44 (203) 681 2756

Email for new applications and general

enquiries: ICACU@ospt.gov.uk

Internet: www.gov.uk

As set out in the 2003 HCCH Guide to Good Practice on Central Authorities, the designation and establishment of a Central Authority is an obligation under Article 6 of the 1980 Hague Convention. A Central Authority needs to have been designated at the time of ratification or accession to the Convention and be in a position to carry out the obligations and functions of the Convention at the time of entry into force. Every Contracting State to the 1980 Hague Convention requires a Central Authority to effectively carry out the objectives of the

---

[41] Correct as of 1 June 2023.

Convention. Under the auspices of the Lord Chancellor[42] as the Central Authority of England and Wales pursuant to section 3 of the Child Abduction and Custody Act 1985, ICACU[43] derives its functions from the Convention, carrying out duties under the Convention, with the support of the Official Solicitor and Public Trustee.[44]

Though Article 7 *h)* of the Hague Convention has been observed to be 'too vague an obligation',[45] it provides that Central Authorities shall take 'all appropriate measures to provide such administrative arrangements as may be necessary and appropriate to secure the safe return of the child'. Nonetheless, as set out in the Guide to Good Practice, the role of the Central Authority includes co-operating to facilitate the safe return of the child and accompanying parent,[46] to verify that arrangements made with protection and welfare authorities are in place,[47] and take appropriate steps to ensure that conditions are met or undertakings are fulfilled.[48] In essence, their role entails a range of administrative and practical work in

---

[43] https://webarchive.nationalarchives.gov.uk/ukgwa/20120215111849/http://www.justice.gov.uk/guidance/protecting-the-vulnerable/official-solicitor/international-child-abduction-and-contact-unit/central-authority-for-england-and-wales.html last visited 1 June 2023.

[43] The International Child Abduction and Contact Unit.

https://webarchive.nationalarchives.gov.uk/ukgwa/20121002233714/http://www.justice.gov.uk/protecting-the-vulnerable/official-solicitor/international-child-abduction-and-contact-unit> last visited 1 June 2023

[45] Peter Ripley, 'A Defence of the Established Approach to the Grave Risk Exception in the Hague Child Abduction Convention' (2008) 4 (3) Journal of Private International Law 464.

[46] Permanent Bureau of the Hague Conference, 'Guide to Good Practice Child Abduction Convention: Part I – Central Authority Practice' (Jordan Publishing Limited 1980) paras. 3.18-3.21.

[47] ibid, para. 3.20.

[48] ibid, para. 3.21.

facilitating the safe return of children at various stages, pre-proceedings or after.[49]

It is the purpose of the Central Authority to take on the responsibility for the administration and handling of child abduction cases. Where a child has been taken or retained abroad, the applicant seeking the return of the child would begin by applying to the Central Authority where he or she lives, so that an *outgoing* application can be processed and transmitted to the State of refuge/requested State (where the child has been taken to or retained). In this instance, ICACU will deal with the outgoing application. In an abduction into England and Wales, an *incoming* case, having received the application, ICACU would then collect all the relevant information and begin the necessary actions that may include the start of court proceedings to facilitate the recovery of the child. In practice, ICACU instructs a firm from an accredited solicitors referral list to act for the applicant who will then file an application in the High Court.

Pursuant to Article 8 of the 1980 Hague Convention, applications to ICACU would contain, amongst others:

a) Information concerning the identity of the applicant, of the child and of the person alleged to have removed or retained the child;

b) Where available, the date of birth of the child;

c) The grounds on which the applicant's claim for return of the child is based;

P.R Beaumont and P.E McEleavy, *Anton's Private International Law* (3rd edn, W. Green 2011) 842, see generally 842-5 on child abduction in practice; R Schuz, *The Hague Child Abduction Convention: A Critical Analysis* (Hart Publishing 2013).

d) All the available information relating to the whereabouts of the child and the identity of the person with whom the child is presumed to be.

3.4 Funding

In a 1980 Hague Abduction Convention case, section 11 of the Child and Custody Act 1985 makes provision for the grant of legal aid or legal advice and assistance, giving effect to Article 26 of the Convention. Article 26 stipulates that whereas a Central Authority shall bear its own costs 'a Contracting State may, by making a reservation in accordance with Article 42, declare that it shall not be bound to assume any costs referred to in the preceding paragraph resulting from the participation of legal counsel or advisers or from court proceedings, except insofar as those costs may be covered by its system of legal aid and advice'. By virtue of the Legal Aid, Sentencing and Punishment of Offenders Act 2012 ('LASPO'), Schedule 1.

Section 17 of Schedule 1, Part 1 states that:

17(1) Civil legal services provided in relation to—

(a) an application made to the Lord Chancellor under the 1980 European Convention on Child Custody for the recognition or enforcement in England and Wales of a decision relating to the custody of a child;

(b) an application made to the Lord Chancellor under the 1980 Hague Convention in respect of a child who is, or is believed to be, in England and Wales;

When a case is lodged in the English court, an applicant parent from whom a child has been abducted to this country (*incoming cases*) will be awarded public funding from the Legal Aid Agency as of right; legal aid for this purpose is not means tested. Further, although paragraph 17 of

Part 1 provides for legal aid services in international agreements concerning children, including 1980 Hague Convention cases, the legal aid eligibility criteria differs for an applicant, as opposed to a respondent. Practitioners should be aware that respondents are only entitled to merits and means tested legal aid. Means tested would mean that the Legal Aid Agency will consider the financial position of the person. A merits test means that the prospect of success is weighed up.

3.5 Urgency

At the forefront of 1980 Hague return proceedings is the recognition that they are time-sensitive and should be handled swiftly. Article 11 reiterates the need for judicial or administrative authorities of Contracting States to act expeditiously in proceedings for the return of children. If the judicial or administrative authority concerned has not reached a decision within six weeks from the date of commencement of proceedings, the requesting State may ask for a statement of reasons. The importance of expeditious proceedings in Hague child abduction cases is crucial, the same applies to non-Convention cases; however, the integrity of the proceedings should not be sacrificed for expedience. For example, in the expeditious handling of cases and adequate evaluation of the merits of allegations of domestic abuse under the Article 13(1)*b)* exception, a balance must be struck. In the case of *Klentzeris v. Klentzeris* [2007] EWCA Civ 533, the trial judge Kirkwood J balanced time and expediency with conducting the hearing, an approach and decision when challenged at the Court of Appeal was found to be 'unimpeachable'. In this case, following the father's application for the return of the children on 31st January 2007, originating summons were issued on 7th February in England. A directions order followed when the matter came before Bennett J on 22nd February and a trial date was set for 3rd and 4th April. More importantly, despite delays in the father's filing of his affidavit and with the CAFCASS[50] officer's report being a little out of time (29th

---

[50] Children and Family Court Advisory and Support Service.

March), the matter proceeded on the trial date which included oral evidence from the CAFCASS officer. Appraising the case management and notwithstanding the delays, the Court of Appeal considered it 'plainly in good enough time for the case that opened on 3 April'.[51] The matter was dealt with within 6 weeks of its first appearance at court, with the assistance of a rigorous case management process.

In summary, practitioners should be mindful of the legal framework and case management system fostered by provisions under the Family Procedural Rules, Part 12, Chapter 6; Practice Direction 12 F; and the President's Guide on Case Management and Mediation of International Child Abduction Proceedings 2023. These are designed to support the swift and summary nature of Hague Convention proceedings, in addition to Practice Direction 12 D in non-Convention proceedings.

---

[51] *Klentzeris v. Klentzeris* [2007] EWCA Civ 533 [8].

CHAPTER FOUR

PRELIMINARY POINTS UNDER ARTICLE 3

4.1 Habitual Residence

Pursuant to Article 4, the Hague Convention applies to a child who is habitually resident in the requesting State prior to the breach of rights of custody or access. Thus, at the core of Hague Convention proceedings is establishing that the State seeking the return of the child is indeed the State of habitual residence. While the 1980 Hague Convention does not offer a definition, leading authorities have settled the law on habitual residence and these definitions apply to both Convention and non-Convention cases. Where the English court is concerned, it has been reiterated time and time again that habitual residence is a question of fact, one that is focused on the child's situation, where other factors such as the parents' purposes and intentions merely being an additional consideration.

In the Court of Appeal case of *M (Children) (Habitual Residence: 1980 Hague Child Abduction Convention)* [2020] EWCA Civ 1105, Moylan LJ highlighted previous guidance on habitual residence, reiterating leading authorities including Lady Hale's dictum in the matter of *A v A and another (Children: Habitual Residence) (Reunite International Child Abduction Centre and others intervening* [2014] [2013] UKSC 60, [2014 A.C. 1. Judgments have continued to approve the formulation of habitual residence, see for example, the Supreme Court decisions *in the matter of B (A Child)* [2016] UKSC, *Re B (A Child: Custody Rights, Habitual Residence)* [2016] EWHC 2174 (Fam) and [2016]; *AR v RN* [2015] UKSC 35 and *Re KL (Abduction: Habitual Residence: Inherent Jurisdiction)* [2013] UKSC 75; and *In re C and another (Children)*

(International Centre for Family Law, Policy and Practice intervening) [2019] AC 1.

Moylan J's dicta at para. 45 of *M (Children)* provides that:

> It has been established for some time that the correct approach to the issue of habitual residence is the same as that adopted by the Court of Justice of the European Union ("CJEU"). Accordingly, in *A v A*, at [48], Lady Hale quoted from the operative part of the CJEU's judgment in *Proceedings brought by A* [2010] Fam 42, at p.69:
>
>> "2. The concept of 'habitual residence' under article 8(1) of Council Regulation (EC) No 2201/2003 must be interpreted as meaning that it corresponds to the place which reflects some degree of integration by the child in a social and family environment. To that end, in particular the duration, regularity, conditions and reasons for the stay on the territory of a member state and the family's move to that state, the child's nationality, the place and conditions of attendance at school, linguistic knowledge and the family and social relationships of the child in that state must be taken into consideration. It is for the national court to establish the habitual residence of the child, taking account of all the circumstances specific to each individual case."

In *Re B (A Minor: Habitual Residence)* [2016] EWHC 2174 (Fam), 2016] 4 WLR 156] at paras. 17-18, Hayden J provided a comprehensive approach to habitual residence, combining authorities as follows:

> i) The habitual residence of a child corresponds to the place which reflects some degree of integration by the child in a social and family environment (A v A, adopting the European test).

ii) The test is essentially a factual one which should not be overlaid with legal sub-rules or glosses. It must be emphasised that the factual enquiry must be centred throughout on the circumstances of the child's life that is most likely to illuminate his habitual residence *(A v A, Re KL)*.

iii) In common with the other rules of jurisdiction in Brussels IIR its meaning is 'shaped in the light of the best interests of the child, in particular on the criterion of proximity'. Proximity in this context means 'the practical connection between the child and the country concerned': A v A (para 80(ii)); Re B (para 42) applying *Mercredi v Chaffe* at para 46).

iv) It is possible for a parent unilaterally to cause a child to change habitual residence by removing the child to another jurisdiction without the consent of the other parent *(Re R)*;

v) A child will usually but not necessarily have the same habitual residence as the parent(s) who care for him or her *(Re LC)*. The younger the child the more likely the proposition, however, this is not to eclipse the fact that the investigation is child focused. It is the child's habitual residence which is in question and, it follows the child's integration which is under consideration.

vi) Parental intention is relevant to the assessment, but not determinative *(Re KL, Re R* and *Re B)*;

vii) It will be highly unusual for a child to have no habitual residence. Usually, a child lose a pre-existing habitual residence at the same time as gaining a new one *(Re B)*; (emphasis added);

viii) In assessing whether a child has lost a pre-existing habitual residence and gained a new one, the court must weigh up the degree of connection which the child had with the state in which he resided before the move (*Re B – see in particular the guidance at para 46);*

ix) It is the **stability** of a child's residence as opposed to its *permanence* which is relevant, though this is qualitative and not quantitative, in the sense that it is the integration of the child into the environment rather than a mere measurement of the time a child spends there *(Re R and earlier in Re KL and Mercredi);*

x) The relevant question is whether a child has achieved **some degree** *of* integration in social and family environment; it is not necessary for a child to be *fully* integrated before becoming habitually resident *(Re R)* (emphasis added);

xi) The requisite degree of integration can, in certain circumstances, develop quite quickly (Art 9 of BIIR envisages within 3 months). It is possible to acquire a new habitual residence in a single day *(A v A; Re B)*. In the latter case Lord Wilson referred (para 45) those *'first roots'* which represent the requisite degree of integration and which a child will *'probably'* put down *'quite quickly'* following a move;

xii) Habitual residence was a question of fact focused upon the situation of the child, with the purposes and intentions of the parents being merely among the relevant factors. It was the stability of the residence that was important, not whether it was of a permanent character. There was no requirement that the child should have been resident in the country in question for a particular period of time, let alone that there should be an intention on the part of one or both parents to reside there permanently or indefinitely (Re R).

xiii) The structure of Brussels IIa, and particularly Recital 12 to the Regulation, demonstrates that it is in a child's best interests to have an habitual residence and accordingly that it would be highly unlikely, albeit possible (or, to use the term adopted in certain parts of the judgment, exceptional), for a child to have no habitual residence; As such, "if interpretation of the concept of habitual residence can reasonably yield both a conclusion that a child has an habitual residence and, alternatively, a conclusion that he lacks any habitual residence, the court should adopt the former" (Re B supra);

18. If there is one clear message emerging both from the European case law and from the Supreme Court, it is that the child is at the centre of the exercise when evaluating his or her habitual residence. This will involve a real and detailed consideration of (inter alia): the child's day to day life and experiences; family environment; interests and hobbies; friends etc. and an appreciation of which adults are most important to the child. The approach must always be child driven. I emphasise this because all too frequently and this case is no exception, the statements filed focus predominantly on the adult parties. It is all too common for the Court to have to drill deep for information about the child's life and routine. This should have been mined to the surface in the preparation of the case and regarded as the primary objective of the statements. I am bound to say that if the lawyers follow this approach more assiduously, I consider that the very discipline of the preparation is most likely to clarify where the child is habitually resident. I must also say that this exercise, if properly engaged with, should lead to a reduction in these enquiries in the courtroom. Habitual residence is

essentially a factual issue, it ought therefore, in the overwhelming majority of cases, to be readily capable of identification by the parties. Thus:

i) The solicitors charged with preparation of the statements must familiarise themselves with the recent case law which emphasises the scope and ambit of the enquiry when assessing habitual residence, (para 17 above maybe a convenient summary);

ii) If the statements do not address the salient issues, counsel, if instructed, should bring the failure to do so to his instructing solicitors attention;

iii) An application should be made expeditiously to the Court for leave to file an amended statement, even though that will inevitably result in a further statement in response;

iv) Lawyers specialising in these international children cases, where the guiding principle is international comity and where the jurisdiction is therefore summary, have become unfamiliar, in my judgement, with the forensic discipline involved in identifying and evaluating the practical realities of children's lives. They must relearn these skills if they are going to be in a position to apply the law as it is now clarified.

The simple message must get through to those who prepare the statements that habitual residence of a child is all about his or her life and not about parental dispute. It is a factual exploration.

Indeed, practitioners should take heed of the guidance of Hayden J in *Re B (a minor)* especially at paragraph 18. It has also been possible for a court to find that the children did not have a country of habitual residence for a period of time (see for example *Re R v B (Stranded: Habitual Residence: Forum Conveniens* [2020] [EWHC] 1041 (Fam)). Further, in *re LC (Children) (Reunite International Child Abduction Centre intervening)* [2014] UKSC 1, important observations were made on the need to assess the 'nature and quality" of the residence and 'whether there was some degree of integration by her (or him) in a social and family environment'. Sufficient degree did not equate to a full degree and a lot will rest on the evidence before the court. In this respect, practitioners will need to be alert to the evidential value that may be placed on independent evidence to demonstrate some degree of integration. In *re LC* it was also found that in determining whether a sufficient degree of integration had been achieved, the state of mind of an adolescent child may be relevant. On this note, it would appear that the approach to habitual residence does combine the parental intentions and child-centred approach. The CJEU decision of *Mercredi* v *Chaffe*[52] played an important role in addressing the distinction between a child's temporary or intermittent presence and habitual residence demonstrated by some degree of integration in a social or family environment. In summary, the decision in *Mercredi* looked at jurisdiction and the definition of 'habitual residence'[53] from the Brussels IIa perspective, which, at the time took precedence over the 1980 Hague Convention as between States to which the Regulation applied. Indeed, establishing social integration is not always possible, especially for a newborn baby, the court addresses this in *B v H (Habitual Residence: Wardship)* [2002] 1 FLR 388.

---

[52] (Case: *C-497/10 PPU)* Judgment of ECJ dated 22nd December 2010 [2011] 1 FLR 1293.

[53] Re A (Case C-523/07) [2009] 2 FLR – CJEU gives a previous definition of 'habitual residence.'

4.2 Unlawful Removal or Retention

In *Re H (Minors) (Abduction: Custody Rights)*, In *re S (Minors) (Abduction: Custody Rights)* [1991] 2 AC 476, [at 500B] Lord Brandon of Oakbrook explained the meaning and scope of unlawful removal or retention as follows:

> For the purposes of the Convention, removal occurs when a child, which has previously been in the State of its habitual residence, is taken away across the frontier of that State; whereas retention occurs where a child, which has previously been for a limited period of time outside the State of its habitual residence, is not returned to that State on the expiry of such limited period.

As the purpose of the 1980 Hague Convention is to protect children from wrongful removal and retention internationally, the removal or retention has to have taken place outside the State. Each event is distinct from the other as they occur on a specific occasion (see also *Re B (a minor) (abduction)* [1995] 2 FCR 505).[54] Thus, removal occurs when a child is taken across the borders of his or her country of habitual residence. Although removal is not a continuing act, it can occur more than once. For instance, where the child is removed from their country of habitual residence, is returned and removed again.[55]

Where retention is concerned, a child's lawful removal may lead to an unlawful retention beyond the date of agreement. 'Retention is not to be construed semantically, but purposively and widely'; therefore, the retention concerns not just the active restrain on the part of the 'taking' parent but also juridical orders obtained on that parent's initiative which

---

[54] [1995] 2 FCR 505; *Re S (a minor) (abduction: European and Hague Conventions)* [1997] 1 FCR 588.

[55] [1998] 1 FCR 17, [1998] 1 FLR 651.

have the effect of frustrating the child's return'.[56] Notably, whereas in *Re H, In re S,* Lord Brandon stated that removal and retention are mutually exclusive events, Macur J in *RS v KS (Abduction: Wrongful Retention)*[57] held that this was not necessarily so. Wrongful retention may include wrongful removal. In the latter case,[58] the father had agreed that the child could leave Lithuania with his mother for a short holiday in England, but the mother had already decided before leaving Lithuania not to return the child. The father's consent to the trip had been obtained by deceit and was therefore vitiated. However, the real wrong carried out by the mother had been to retain the child beyond the agreed date of his return and this unlawful retention amounted to an unlawful removal. Another concept that practitioners should be aware of is 'repudiatory retention'. In 2018, the Supreme Court in *Re C (Children) (Rev 1)* [2018] UKSC 8 determined that 'repudiatory retention' is possible in law,[59] a concept that may well create a tension with the question of habitual residence. Nonetheless, repudiatory retention considers 'whether the travelling parent has manifested a denial, or repudiation, of the rights of the left-behind parent'.[60] Though a 'non-exhaustive definition', Lord Hughes went on to set down markers of repudiatory retention at paragraph 51 (i)-(v). In summary: that there is a subjective intention not to return the child, a once internal thought demonstrated by '...some objectively identifiable act or statement, or combination of such, which manifests the denial, or repudiation, of the rights of custody of the left-behind parent. A declaration of intent to a third party might suffice, but a privately formed decision would not, without more, do so', and that the repudiation need not necessarily be communicated to the left-behind parent.

---

[56] *Re B (minors) (abduction) (No 1 and 2)* [1993] 1 FLR 993.

[57] [2009] 2 FLR 1231.

[58] ibid.

[59] See also *In re S (Minors) (Abductions: Wrongful Retention)* [1994] Fam 70.

[60] *Re C (Children) (Rev 1)* [2018] UKSC 8, para. 51.

4.3 Rights of Custody vs Rights of Access

Article 3 of the Convention provides that: -

> The removal or the retention of a child is to be considered wrongful where -
>
> *a)* it is in breach of rights of custody attributed to a person, an institution, or any other body, either jointly or alone, under the law of the State in which the child was habitually resident immediately before the removal or retention; and
>
> *b)* at the time of removal or retention those rights were actually exercised, either jointly or alone, or would have been so exercised but for the removal or retention.
>
> The rights of custody mentioned in sub-paragraph *a)* above, may arise in particular by operation of law or by reason of a judicial or administrative decision, or by reason of an agreement having legal effect under the law of that State.

Article 5 provides a partial autonomous definition but also points out the distinction between rights of custody and rights of access:

For the purposes of this Convention -

> *a)* 'rights of custody' shall include rights relating to the care of the person of the child and, in particular, the right to determine the child's place of residence;
>
> *b)* 'rights of access' shall include the right to take a child for a limited period of time to a place other than the child's habitual residence.

Establishing rights of custody is important as it represents an identifiable legal link between an individual and the child. Therefore, if that right is breached, the legally responsible parent who has been disadvantaged will be able to petition for its restoration. Moreover, it further supports the status quo that it is in the interest of a child to be returned to a 'home' environment and in some cases to be reunited with his primary carer. There therefore lies a correlative relationship between protecting one's custody right from being breached and protecting the interests of the abducted child.

Where case law is concerned, see for example *Re D (A Child) (Abduction: Rights of Custody)* [2006] UKHL 51, [2007] 1 AC 619, [2007] 1 All ER 783, [2007] 1 FLR 961 at paragraph 37 in particular, with reference to *In re H (A Minor) (Abduction: Rights of Custody)* [2000] 2 AC 291. The Guide on Transfrontier Contact explains that, in the context of the 1980 Hague Convention, rights of custody should generally be regarded as including rights of access/contact (where Article 21 is concerned). Practice Direction 12F, paragraph 2.16 further defines rights of custody as meaning rights relating to the care of the person of the child and in particular the right to determine the child's place of residence. This effectively translates to parental responsibility. However, note that the English courts are bound to accept the meaning of rights of custody pursuant to the foreign laws of the child's State of habitual residence. Custody rights may arise by operation of law (*ex lege*), by reason of a judicial or administrative decisions or by reasons of an agreement having legal effect under the law of the State in which the child was habitually residence immediately before the removal or retention. Of note, the Convention does not limit reference to the internal rules of foreign law, thereby denoting reference to the choice of law rules of the State of the child's habitual residence, in essence, in accordance with the doctrine of *renvoi*.

In relation to Article 5(b) on effective exercise of rights of access, the partial definition has also been problematic for jurisdictions. Nevertheless, it would be appropriate to consider access rights as contact rights whilst appreciating that a parent with or seeking access rights may also hold custody rights or as it may be referred to: *patria potestas.* In *Valcheva v Babanarakis* [2018] 1 FLR 1571 [33-34, 37], which concerned a grandmother's wish to exercise rights of access, it was held that defining access rights should be understood 'as referring not only to the rights of access of parents to their child, but also to the rights of access of other persons with whom it is important for the child to maintain a personal relationship, among others, that child's grandparents, whether or not they are holders of parental responsibility'. Further exploration as to rights of access is considered alongside Articles 7 and 21 of the Convention below.

4.4 The 'Standing' to Apply: Inchoate Custody Rights

This section delves further into Article 5 of the 1980 Hague Convention, shedding light on how a legal practitioner might approach the issue of inchoate custody rights, see for example: *Re H. (Abduction: Rights of Custody)* [2000] 1 FLR 374, *Re K (Abduction: Inchoate Rights)* [2014] UKSC 29, and *NM v SM* [2017] EWHC 1294 (Fam).

With the steady picture of majority abductions being committed by mothers who are therefore the *respondents* in return proceedings, conversely fathers are by and large, the *applicants.* In cases of unmarried fathers (and those without parental responsibility) or non-custodial relatives even, the question arises as to how to approach applicants who have actively cared for removed or retained children. Wherein without possessing legal custody rights, the question is whether so called 'inchoate custody rights' may apply. The Convention provides that the person making the application should have custody rights and for an unmarried father this means either through parental responsibility (agreed or named on the birth certificate, or by court order) or by way of an application already lodged with the court. As already noted, Article 3 provides that a right of custody may arise by operation of law or by reason of a judicial or administrative decision, or by an agreement having legal effect.

Following the cases of *Re C (a minor) (abduction) and C v C (minor: abduction: rights of custody abroad)*, [61] the Special Commission concluded in its second meeting concerning the operation of the Hague Convention that:

> 'The key concepts which determine the scope of the Hague Convention are not dependent for their meaning on any single legal system. Thus, the expression "rights of custody", for example, does not coincide with any particular concept of custody in a domestic law, but draws its meaning from the definitions, structure, and purpose of the Hague Convention'.[62]

Having rights of custody is an important element in order that where the mother does remove the child, it would be a breach of that right and gives father the standing to make an application under the Hague Convention. For example, the position of an unmarried father as held in *Re J (A Minor) (Abduction: Custody Rights)*[63] is that he had no rights of custody capable of being breached. Therefore, it is for the court to determine whether a father's rights amount to 'rights of custody' within the meaning of the Hague Convention. The case of *Re W; Re B (Child Abduction; Unmarried Father)*[64] provides helpful guidance as to the circumstances in which an unmarried father should be advised that removal by the mother of a child who is habitually resident in England and Wales will be wrongful under

---

[61] [1989] FCR 197 at 207-208; *sub nom C v C (minor: abduction: rights of custody abroad)* [1989] 2 All ER 465 at 472-473, [1989] 1 WLR 654 at 663.

[62] Permanent Bureau of the Hague Conference, Report of the Second Special Commission Meeting to Review the Operation of the Hague Convention on the Civil Aspects of International Child Abduction, 18-21 January 1993.

[63] [1990] 2 AC 562. A case, in fact decided under Western Australian law, but the principles would be the same under English law.

[64] [1998] 2 FLR 146.

the Hague Convention. Baroness Hale in her judgment notes that these include where:

(a) The father has parental responsibility either by agreement or by court order; or

(b) There is a court order in force prohibiting removal; or

(c) There are relevant proceedings pending in a court in England and Wales; or

(d) The father is currently the primary carer for the child, at least if the mother has delegated such care to him.

In addition, *Re S (Abduction: Hague and European Conventions)*[65] has established that a father may also have rights of custody where he has interim care and control of the child in wardship proceedings.[66] In respect of paragraph (d) above, it is important to note that the father should have de facto care of the child and not mere contact, however extensive, as the court has drawn a distinction between strict legal rights and de facto or 'inchoate' rights.[67] Aside from fathers without custody rights, the picture has expanded to other circumstances where inchoate rights of custody might arise. As per the Supreme Court decision in *Re K (Abduction: Inchoate Rights)* [2014] UKSC 29, the court allowed the appeal of a grandmother, finding that she had 'rights of custody' for the purposes of the 1980 Hague Convention (and *Brussels IIa*[68] – as it then was, would have applied).

---

[65] [1997] 1 FLR 958.

[66] Section 12(1) of the Children Act 1989.

[67] *Re B (A Minor) (Abduction)* [1994] 2 FLR 249: Peter Gibson LJ; factual care of the child could give rise to 'rights of custody'.

[68] Council Regulation (EC) No 2201/2003 of 27 November 2003 concerning jurisdiction and the recognition and enforcement of judgments in matrimonial matters and the matters of parental responsibility, repealing

The applicant must also demonstrate that his or her rights of custody which have allegedly been breached were actually exercised at the time of the removal or retention or would have been so if the child had not been abducted. Otherwise, the respondent taking parent would no doubt have grounds to challenge the application for return on the basis of Article 13(1)(a). For legal practitioners, a factual exercise of ascertaining the nature of the relationship between the child(dren) and left behind parent should offer clarity on this point.

Regulation (EC) No 1347/2000, now repealed by Council Regulation (EC) No 2019/1111 of 25 June 2019 on jurisdiction, the recognition and enforcement of decisions in matrimonial matters and the matters of parental responsibility, and on international child abduction (recast) with entry into force on 1 August 2022 (referred to as 'Brussels IIter' or 'the Recast Regulation')).

CHAPTER FIVE

PLEADING AN
EXCEPTION
TO RETURN

To *defend* a Hague summary return application is to rely on one of the exceptions to return contained in the 1980 Hague Convention. The Explanatory Report acknowledges that 'the removal of the child can sometimes be justified by objective reasons which have to do either with its person, or the environment with which it is most closely connected'.[69] Thus, alongside the Convention's objectives are 'exceptions' to the duty to secure the prompt return of the child, where a departure from the principles may be justified. These are: Article 12(2) child settlement in their new environment; Article 13(1) (a) non-exercise of the rights of custody by the left behind parent or other person with parental responsibility, consent, acquiescence; Article 13(1)*b)* a grave risk of physical harm, psychological harm, or other intolerable situation; Article 13(2) the child's objections; and Article 20 fundamental principles relating to the protection of human rights and fundamental freedoms. It is critical to know and understand your client's case from the outset. It is the foundation for clear and cogent pleadings (such as witness statements, the respondents' answer), and will help dictate and focus any evidential exercise.

---

[69] Perez-Vera Report, para. 25.

5.1 Settlement (Article 12)

Article 12(2) provides that:

> 'The judicial or administrative authority, even where the proceedings have been commenced after the expiration of the period of one year [...], shall also order the return of the child, unless it is demonstrated that the child is now settled in its new environment'.

When a child is removed or retained, and less than 12 months have elapsed before the commencement of proceedings, then the child is to be returned forthwith (Art 12(1)). Even if more than twelve months have elapsed, the court may exercise its discretion and order the return of the child, unless it is demonstrated that the child is now settled in their new environment (Art 12(2)). The taking parent bears the burden of establishing that the child is now settled in that State. Where a wrongful removal or retention is established, the courts are bound to order that child's immediate return to the State of his habitual residence. Even though the child is now settled, the power under Article 18 does not limit the power of a judicial or administrative authority to order the return of a child at any time. If a return is ordered, then any other custody order ceases to have effect, but if refused, the court can hear any other application upon its merits.[70]

The exercise of the court's discretion to order a return and Article 12 is considered in great depth in the case of *Re O (Children)* [2011] EWCA Civ 128 amongst other important points raised. The facts of the case are as follows: the mother and father originated from Nigeria but met in the United States. The children and the father had dual US and Nigerian

---

[70] N Lowe and G Douglas, *Bromley's Family Law* Ninth Edition. Butterworths, 1998, p. 498. Child Abduction and Custody Act 1985 s25 and Article 16. 'Custody Orders' includes 8 orders under the Children Act 1989: Child Abduction and Custody Act 1985, Sch. 3.

citizenship. In February 2009 the mother took the children to Nigeria for a holiday and subsequently informed the father that she intended to stay in Nigeria with the children. The father swiftly issued proceedings in the United States for the return of the children. The father also issued an application in the US courts for sole custody of the children. In that application he misled the court about the children's whereabouts and his contact with the children. In November 2009 the father issued proceedings in Nigeria. In July 2010 the mother and children came to England for a holiday. The father made an application under the 1980 Hague Convention and the mother and children were prohibited from leaving the UK. The father sought the return of the children to the US. The mother relied on Articles 13(a), 13(1)*b)* and 12. The judge found that the proceedings had commenced more than 12 months after the wrongful retention and the children were 'settled' in Nigeria. He rejected the mother's other defences. Having found the children settled in Nigeria, the judge nonetheless decided to exercise his discretion to return the children to the US. The mother appealed this decision.

In the Court of Appeal, Black LJ, giving the lead judgment, upheld the mother's appeal. *Re M and another* is the leading authority on this point. The Hague Convention policy factors are only one consideration when deciding whether to return children: they are not to be given overriding significance but 'their relevance is strictly as part of the whole picture.'[71] The immediate needs and general welfare of the children must also be taken into account. It was found that the judge had erred in failing to apply the principles in *Re M and another* and insofar as he had considered the children's welfare, had adopted a generalised approach rather than considering the individual circumstances of the children. The Court of Appeal went on to determine the question of whether the children, being settled in Nigeria, should be returned to the US. It was determined that the mother and children should be allowed to remain in Nigeria. The factors cited as being relevant to this decision were:

---

[71] ibid, para. 24.

a) *The case was far from being a 'hot pursuit' one and the policy considerations were not as prominent as they might be;*

b) *At no point had the mother concealed the children's whereabouts from the father;*

c) *The children did not view the US as their home;*

d) *Both parents were very familiar with Nigeria and the father had previously had contact with the children there. Many other maternal and paternal relatives (including another child of the father) lived in Nigeria;*

e) *The Nigerian courts were already seised of the matter and were a more appropriate jurisdiction than the US courts;*

f) *The father's immoderate and underhand behaviour since Spring 2009 meant it would be much easier for the mother to cope with the ongoing dispute if she was in Nigeria with the support of her family.*

As to the issue of concealment, see *Cannon v Cannon* [2005] 1 WLR 32 where judges were reminded that they 'should not apply a rigid rule of disregard but they should look critically at any alleged settlement that is built on concealment and deceit, especially if the defendant is a fugitive from criminal justice'.

5.2 Consent or Acquiescence (Article 13(1)(a))

Article 13(1)(a) provides that:

> 'Notwithstanding the provisions of the preceding Article, the judicial or administrative authority of the requested State is not bound to order the return of the child if the person,

institution, or other body which opposes its return establishes that –

a) the person, institution or other body having the care of the person of the child was not actually exercising the custody rights at the time of removal or retention, or had consented to or subsequently acquiesced in the removal or retention; [...]'

Lord Justice Ward in *Re P-J (Children) (Abduction: Consent)* [2009] EWCA Civ 588 [2010] 1 WLR 1237, sets out the applicable principles relating to the law on consent as follows [48]:

'In my judgment, the following principles should be deduced from these authorities.

(i) Consent to the removal of the child must be clear and unequivocal.

(ii) Consent can be given to the removal at some future but unspecified time or upon the happening of some future event.

(iii) Such advance consent must, however, still be operative and in force at the time of the actual removal.

(iv) The happening of the future event must not have been expressed in terms which are too vague or uncertain for both parties to know whether the condition will be fulfilled. Fulfilment of the condition must not depend on the subjective determination of one party, for example, 'Whatever you may think, I have concluded that the marriage has broken down and so I am free to leave with the child'. The event must be objectively verifiable.

(v) Consent, or lack of it, must be viewed in the context of the realities of family life, or more precisely, in the context of the realities of the disintegration of family life. It is not to be viewed in the context of nor governed by the law of contract.

(vi) Consequently, consent can be withdrawn at any time before actual removal. If it is, the proper course if for any dispute about removal to be resolved by the courts of the country of habitual residence before the child is removed.

(vii) The burden of proving the consent rests on him or her who asserts it.

(viii) The inquiry is inevitably fact specific, and the facts and circumstances will vary infinitely from case to case.

(ix) The ultimate question is a simple one even if a multitude of facts bear upon the answer. It is simply this: had the other parent clearly and unequivocally consented to the removal?"

In the recent decision of *G (Abduction Consent discretion)* [2021] EWCA Civ 139 [25], the Court of Appeal reiterated that:

(1) The removing parent must prove consent to the civil standard. The inquiry is fact-specific, and the ultimate question is: had the remaining parent clearly and unequivocally consented to the removal?

(2) The presence or absence of consent must be viewed in the context of the common sense realities of family life and family breakdown, and not in the context of the law of contract. The court will focus on the reality of the family's situation and consider all the circumstances in making its assessment. A primary focus is likely to be on the words and actions of the remaining parent. The words and actions of

the removing parent may also be a significant indicator of whether that parent genuinely believed that consent had been given, and consequently an indicator of whether consent had in fact been given.

(3) Consent must be clear and unequivocal, but it does not have to be given in writing or in any particular terms. It may be manifested by words and/or inferred from conduct.

(4) A person may consent with the gravest reservations, but that does not render the consent invalid if the evidence is otherwise sufficient to establish it.

(5) Consent must be real in the sense that it relates to a removal in circumstances that are broadly within the contemplation of both parties.

(6) Consent that would not have been given but for some material deception or misrepresentation on the part of the removing parent will not be valid.

(7) Consent must be given before removal. Advance consent may be given to removal at some future but unspecified time or upon the happening of an event that can be objectively verified by both parties. To be valid, such consent must still be operative at the time of the removal.

(8) Consent can be withdrawn at any time before the actual removal. The question will be whether, in the light of the words and/or conduct of the remaining parent, the previous consent remained operative or not.

(9) The giving or withdrawing of consent by a remaining parent must have been made known by words and/or conduct to the removing parent. A consent or withdrawal of

consent of which a removing parent is unaware cannot be effective.

The comprehensive guidance on consent is demonstrated above, with further case law such as *Re L (Abduction: Future Consent)* [2007] EWHC 2181 (Fam); [2008] 1 FLR 914 (Bodey J), *In re K (Abduction: Consent)* [1997] 2 FLR 212 (Lady Hale) and *Re M (Abduction) (Consent: Acquiescence)* [1999] 1 FLR. 174 (Wall J).

Where Acquiescence is concerned, it is helpful to observe the principles summarised in *Re H. and Others (Minors) (Abduction: Acquiescence)* [1998] AC 72 [90e-g] by Lord Browne-Wilkinson:

> "To bring these strands together, in my view the applicable principles are as follows:
>
> (1) For the purposes of Article 13 of the Convention, the question whether the wronged parent has "acquiesced" in the removal or retention of the child depends upon his actual state of mind. As Neill L.J. said in *In re S. (Minors)* "the court is primarily concerned, not with the question of the other parent's perception of the applicant's conduct, but with the question whether the applicant acquiesced in fact".
>
> (2) The subjective intention of the wronged parent is a question of fact for the trial judge to determine in all the circumstances of the case, the burden of proof being on the abducting parent.
>
> (3) The trial judge, in reaching his decision on that question of fact, will no doubt be inclined to attach more weight to the contemporaneous words and actions of the wronged parent than to his bare assertions in evidence of his intention. But that is a question of the weight to be attached to evidence and is not a question of law.

(4) There is only one exception. Where the words or actions of the wronged parent clearly and unequivocally show and have led the other parent to believe that the wronged parent is not asserting or going to assert his right to the summary return of the child and are inconsistent with such return, justice requires that the wronged parent be held to have acquiesced.'

Accordingly, in a case of alleged acquiescence, it is also a matter of fact, and not a question of law. The court will be seeking to ascertain the subjective intentions of the left behind parent, with clearly visible and outward acts or expressed words would be more compelling than seeking to make assertions of his or her subsequent intentions.

5.3 The Grave Risk of Harm (Article 13(1)*b*))

Article 13 (1)*b)* is arguably one of, if not the most litigated 1980 Hague Convention exceptions. It is hoped that this section will guide practitioners through a snapshot of evolving, though not exhaustive, case law from the English Court's perspective, especially where allegations of domestic violence and abuse[72] are raised. As such, this section will highlight key principles and knowledge through case law analysis.

---

[72] Article 3(b) of the Council of Europe Convention on Preventing and Combating Violence Against Women and Domestic Violence, Istanbul, 11.v.2011 provides a wide definition of domestic violence: acts of physical, sexual, psychological, and economic violence that occur within the family or domestic unit or between former or current spouses or partners, whether or not the perpetrator shares or has shared the same residence with the victim. Without seeking to introduce an exhaustive range of abusive behaviours, abuse also extends to financial control, a pattern of coercive control such as intimidation, humiliation, isolation from sources of support and means of independence, stalking, gaslighting/mind games, emotional abuse, inducing fear and online abuse. Other consequential

Article 13 (1)*b)* provides that:

> Notwithstanding the provisions of the preceding Article, the judicial or administrative authority of the requested State is not bound to order the return of the child if the person, institution, or other body which opposes its return establishes that –
>
> *b)* there is a grave risk that his or her return would expose the child to physical or psychological harm or otherwise place the child in an intolerable situation.

As articulated by Dyer, the specificity of the provisions contained in the Hague Convention 'intrudes upon the jurisdiction of the courts in the country to which the child has been taken',[73] and when those courts are tasked with addressing the tension between applying the Hague Convention restrictively and examining the factual matrix of grounds under the Article 13(1)*b)* exception, it is understandable as to why the dimension would cause uncertainties. Despite the discussions contained in the *Procès-verbal* and the Explanatory Report, the terminology used in Article 13(1)*b)* appears to invite a range of interpretations within an overall 'strict' construction of the exception to the duty to return the child. Where the English Court is concerned, evoking Article 13(1)*b)*, like all other 'defences', does not guarantee that the child's return will be refused as the courts have to be satisfied that protective measures would not be available, suitable, or adequate to ameliorate the risk identified. When preparing or putting their client's case, practitioners must be cognizant of the fact that the grave risk of harm is about the child, not the parent, so that even when the facts relied upon inextricably engage

---

aspects of domestic violence include Battered Woman Syndrome and Post Separation Violence.

[73] Adair Dyer, 'The Hague Convention on the Civil Aspects of International Child Abduction – Towards Global Cooperation, Its Successes, and Failures' (1993) 1 (3) The International Journal of Children's Rights, 273.

the welfare or circumstances of the parent, the effect on the child has to be articulated. In *TB v JB (Abduction: Grave_Risk of Harm)* [2000] EWCA Civ 337; [2001] 2 FLR 515, [44] Baroness Hale also stated that:

> "It is important to remember that the risks in question are those faced by the children, not by the parent. But those risks may be quite different depending upon whether they are returning to the home country where the primary carer is the 'left behind' parent or whether they are returning to a home country where their primary carer will herself face severe difficulties in providing properly for their needs. Primary carers who have fled from abuse and maltreatment should not be expected to go back to it if this will have a seriously detrimental effect upon the children. We are now more conscious of the effects of such treatment, not only on the immediate victims but also on the children who witness it."

Case law has demonstrated that the grave risk burden is often difficult to discharge. Nevertheless, the necessity for a strict approach, but with no extra gloss,[74] is self-evident. This is because the summary return mechanism of the 1980 Hague Convention cannot function properly if proceedings automatically become embroiled in a detailed investigation as to the well-being of a child. Having said that, there is a distinction between applying the 1980 Hague Convention strictly and restrictively. Where the latter is concerned, practitioners should be mindful of instances where it appears that the court is setting the bar too high. For example, in relation to the grave risk of intolerability, in *Re D (A Child)* [2006] UKHL 51-52 Baroness Hale stated that the English courts may have set the bar too high, that 'intolerable' is a strong word, but when applied to a child must mean 'a situation which this particular child in these particular circumstances should not be expected to tolerate'.

---

[74] *Re E (Children) (Abduction: Custody Appeal)* [2011] UKSC 27 [52].

According to the HCCH Guide to Good Practice on Article 13(1)*b)*, whether it be physical, psychological, other intolerable situation or a combination, the risk must be real and of a level of seriousness to constitute grave. The words 'physical or psychological harm' are not qualified; however, they 'gain colour' from the third limb of the defence – or other 'intolerable situation' (*Re E (Children)* [2011] UKSC 27). The overly strict approach on the interpretation of the grave risk of harm such as requiring a very high degree of intolerability has been rejected (see for example *Re A (Minors) (Abduction: Custody Rights)* [1992] Fam 106, [1992] 1 All ER 929). As Baroness Hale reminded the court in *Re E (Children)* the exception to return did not need 'any extra interpretation or gloss' (para 52), Article 13(1)*b)* should be applied 'sensibly' (para 81) to a child's individual circumstances.

5.3.1 Domestic Abuse Allegations Pursuant to Article 13(1)*b)*

It is now widely accepted and acknowledged that children exposed to domestic abuse do not have to be directly targeted to be victims.[75] Witnessing domestic violence alone is sufficiently traumatising to cause harm to children. As stated by Schuz, where a non-return order is made in cases involving serious domestic violence, it would 'broadcast the message that violence does not pay'.[76] A child being a direct victim of domestic abuse may be harm directed at the child such as physical, emotional, sexual or any other form of coercive or controlling behaviour towards the child; or indirectly suffering psychological harm from witnessing abuse (spousal abuse or intimate partner violence). It is necessary to point out that children who have suffered harm perpetrated directly towards them, e.g., physical, or sexual harm, are also likely to

---

[75] Council of Europe Treaty Series 210, 'Explanatory Report to the Council of Europe Convention on Preventing and Combating Violence Against Women and Domestic Violence, Istanbul, 11.v.2011, para 27, as well as the Council of Europe Convention on Preventing and Combating Violence Against Women and Domestic Violence, Istanbul, 11.v.2011.

[76] Schuz, p. 314.

endure the indirect consequences of psychological harm. These circumstances are all capable of amounting to a grave risk of harm.

Following the pivotal Supreme Court decisions in *Re E (Children)* [2011] UKSC 27 and *Re S (A Child) (Abduction: Rights of Custody)* [2012] UKSC 10, it is well established that domestic violence perpetrated on a parent can be so harmful so as to constitute a grave risk of harm to a child. The child's exposure to that abuse may be direct or indirect, but even in the latter situation, that too may constitute a grave risk of harm. As cases have continued to evolve post the *Re E (Children), Re S (a Child)* era,[77] practitioners may find useful the UK POAM National Report which sets out a comprehensive appraisal of precedents involving domestic abuse. Of note, *Re E (Children)* at (para 34) reiterated that a child should not be reasonably expected to tolerate 'exposure to the harmful effects of seeing and hearing the physical or psychological abuse of her own parent'. In *Re S (A child) (Abduction: Rights of Custody)* [2012] UKSC 10, the Supreme Court emphasised that 'the critical question is what will happen if, with the mother, the child is returned. If the court concludes that, on return, the mother will suffer such anxieties that their effect on her mental health will create a situation that is intolerable for the child, then the child should not be returned. It matters not whether the mother's anxieties will be reasonable or unreasonable. The extent to which there will, objectively, be good cause for the mother to be anxious on return will nevertheless be relevant to the court's assessment of the mother's mental state if the child is returned.'[78]

In *LS v AS* [2014] EWHC 1626 (Fam) the court declined to make a return order, taking into account the severe and extensive history of

---

[77] K Trimmings and O Momoh (2021) "Intersection between Domestic Violence and International Parental Child Abduction: Protection of Abducting Mothers in Return Proceedings" (2021) 35 International Journal of Law, Policy and the Family 1.

[78] [2012] UKSC 10, para. 34.

violence throughout, the father being described as 'unpredictable, violent and tyrannical' volatility.

> 'I draw from the evidence that domestic violence both physical and verbal has been so much a part of the life experience of these children that its cessation has overwhelmed them and set both their sense of the past and of the possibilities for the future in perspective. The father expresses no understanding of the reasons for his behaviour and his violence is so entrenched (including a conviction for assaulting a nephew) that it is unlikely to be addressed effectively or at all within the timescales of these children." [86] On my evaluation of the evidence I consider this is likely to have occurred frequently in consequence of the father's volatility. [89] All this, it seems to me, is sufficient to identify the factual matrix of the case.'[90]

Leaning on jurisprudence from the European Court of Human Rights, in the case of *Opuz v. Turkey, Application no. 33401/02,* ECHR 2009, the victim of serious acts of violence that was criminally prosecuted withdrew her complaints at key points, under the threat of her husband. The prosecution did not instantly proceed in the public interest, but the victim remained unprotected for months. The ECtHR found that there was a violation of a positive obligation under Article 2 of the ECHR, as the authorities could have ordered protective measures under the relevant legislation, in particular an injunction restraining the husband from contacting, communicating with or approaching the applicant mother or entering defined areas. Although the victim had withdrawn her complaints, once the situation had been brought to the authorities' attention, they could not rely on the victims' attitude for their failure to take adequate measures to prevent threats to physical integrity being carried out (paras 138-149). Practitioners should be alert to the practical realities of the case advanced by their clients and be able to apply forensic rigour in examining the adequacy of protective measures. The nature, frequency and intensity of physical abuse and threats to the mother is such that the harm extends to emotional and psychological abuse, highlighted in the police reports.

The approach to the grave risk of harm exception under Article 13(1)b)

The HCCH Guide to Good Practice on Article 13(1)*b)* provides guidance on approaching the Article 13(1)*b)* grave risk exception, including in cases involving domestic abuse.[79] The Guide highlights that 'as a first step, the court should consider whether the assertions are of such a nature, and of sufficient detail and substance, that they could constitute a grave risk. Broad or general assertions are very unlikely to be sufficient".[80]

After the evaluation of the information or evidence available, the court may then consider protective measures in this manner:

> "Has the person, institution or other body which opposes the child's return (in most cases, the taking parent) satisfied the court that there is a grave risk that the return would expose the child to physical or psychological harm or otherwise place the child in an intolerable situation, taking into account any adequate and effective measures available or in place in the State of habitual residence to protect the child from the grave risk?"[81]

The interpretation and application of Article 13(1)*b)* has, over time, produced two emerging practices. The first is where the English Court assumes the allegations of domestic violence are true and, on that basis, considers whether adequate protective measures exist. This is an approach synonymous to that which was coined in *Re E (Children)* – with the Supreme court neither implicitly endorsing not criticising the

---

[79] HCCH Guide to Good Practice on Article 13(1)*b),* p. 31-33

[80] ibid, p. 31.

[81] ibid, p. 33.

approach. The second approach is whether an evaluative exercise is conducted first to investigate the credibility or merits of the allegations before considering if protective measures can adequately ameliorate the risk identified. The HCCH Guide to Good Practice on Article 13(1)*b)* advocates for the latter approach. Having said that, the language of assuming the risk at its highest is perhaps misleading. This is because in reality, in *Re S (a Chid)* the court did undertake an evaluative exercise. The trial judge considered about 300 text messages and emails passed between the parents, a letter from the mother's GP, a psychologist's report, and a jointly instructed psychiatrist who commented on the mother having suffered from Battered Women Syndrome and acute stress syndrome, and the risk of reoccurrence of her anxiety and depression. It is apparent that the court conducted an exercise akin to investigating the merits of the allegations; finding 'genuine conviction that she [the mother] has been the victim of domestic violence' and accepting the 'fragility of the mother's psychological health'. Indeed, MacDonald J in *Uhd v McKay* [2019] EWHC 1239 (Fam) observed that the Supreme Court dicta in *Re E* by which the court assumes the risk relied upon at its highest is not an exercise that excludes consideration of relevant evidence before the court. MacDonald J expressed that 'the court is not prevented from examining the evidence before it that informs the question of objective risk and evaluating that evidence in a manner consistent with the summary nature of these proceedings.' Whereas in the *matter of C (Children) (Abduction Article 13(b))* [2018] EWCA Civ 2834, LJ Lewison in the Court of Appeal directly rejected the *Re E* approach, did so with great respect but finding it to be 'unprincipled', that simply assuming the allegations at their highest was not sufficient and as it would seem, 'experienced family judges do not apply *Re E in its full rigour'* (paras. 69-70). Further arguments that may be raised against the idea of a purely assumptive exercise include the fact that the Article 6 rights of the left behind parent are in jeopardy and that protective measures are likely to be stereotyped and not in response to a real and specific grave risk that may be identified.

As such, practitioners should be aware of developing authorities post the *Re E* and *Re S* era that endorses an evaluative exercise being conducted as part of the court's approach to the grave risk of harm, especially in cases where allegations of domestic violence have been raised. Recalling Professor Perez-Vera on the exceptions to return, it was observed that they do not apply automatically, and neither should the process towards establishing that risk. In the ECtHR decision of *X v. Latvia [GC] (Application no. 27853/09)* Grand Chamber [2013], the Grand Chamber reiterated the obligation of the Croatian courts to have 'effectively'[82] examined the possible existence of a grave risk pursuant to Article 13(1)*b*). That there was a duty and obligation to 'undertake an effective examination'[83] of allegations made by a party on the basis of one of the exceptions expressly provided for.[84] The Grand Chamber went on to state that the court must satisfy themselves that 'adequate' and 'tangible' protective measures are convincingly provided. In summary, drawing from jurisprudence on this issue, along with the HCCH Guide to Good Practice on Article 13(1)*b*), the approach to the grave risk of harm requires consideration of arguable allegations, where the court, with sufficient detail, makes a ruling giving specific reasons in the light of the circumstances of the case, ensuring that the evaluation is not automatic or stereotyped.[85]

---

[82] *X v. Latvia* [GC] (Application no. 27853/09) Grand Chamber [2013], para. 117, See also O Momoh 'The interpretation and application of Article 13(1)b of the Hague Child Abduction Convention in cases involving domestic violence: Revisiting *X v Latvia* and the principle of "effective examination"' (2019) 15(3) Journal of Private International Law, 626-657.

[83] X v Latvia, 'Concurring Opinion of Judge Pinto De Albuquerque', where effective examination is described as a thorough, limited, and expeditious investigation. Judge Albuquerque suggests that an 'in-depth' judicial enquiry did not have to be obtuse, ill-defined, and self-indulgent.

[84] *X v Latvia,* para. 118.

[85] *X v Latvia,* para. 107.

5.3.2 Child Abduction and Asylum

In *G v G (international child abduction)* [2021] UKSC 9, the Supreme Court considered the intersection[86] between the 1980 Hague Convention and asylum law including, in particular, the 1951 Geneva Convention. This is because whereas the objective of the 1980 Hague Convention is to protect children from the harmful effects of cross border abductions by facilitating their prompt return to the country taken from, the 1951 Geneva Convention seeks to protect refugees from a return to a country where they may be persecuted; a protection from refoulement. In this case, the child, aged 8, had been removed from South Africa to England where the mother, upon arrival, applied for asylum with the child as a dependent. In addressing important questions raised by this interplay, including the principle of non-refoulement in 1980 Hague Convention cases, the Supreme Court set down useful guidance as follows:

> [117] a request for international protection made by a principal applicant naming a child as a dependant is also an application by the child, if objectively it can be understood as such... such an application can (and should) objectively be understood as an application by the child, for a combination of two reasons. The first is the inherent likelihood, expressly recognised in recital (27) to the Qualification Directive (quoted at para 85 above), that any grounds which an adult applicant may raise for fearing persecution or serious harm of a relevant kind will also apply, by reason of their relationship, to a child who is a dependant of that adult. The second is that, as pointed out in the Secretary of State's submissions, in the case of a child, it is the parent applicant who determines, on behalf of their

---

[86] See also *In re H (A Child) (International Abduction: Asylum and Welfare)* [2016] EWCA Civ 988; [2017] 2 FLR 527, *R (A Child) (Asylum and 1980 Hague Convention Application)* [2022] EWCA Civ 188.

child, whether to make a claim for asylum. An omission by a child to make an application in their own right cannot therefore be regarded as a choice which the child has made (even if he or she has legal capacity to make it).

[121] a child named as a dependant on the parent's asylum application and who has not made a separate request for international protection generally can and should be understood to be seeking such protection and therefore treated as an applicant. I would allow this aspect of the appeal.

[122, 130, 134] where the Qualification Directive and the Procedures Directives apply... a dependant who can objectively be understood as being an applicant is entitled to rely on article 7 of the Procedures Directive which ensures non-refoulement of a refugee who is awaiting a decision so that a return order cannot be implemented pending determination by the Secretary of State....an applicant has protection from refoulement pending the determination of that application, so that until the request for international protection is determined by the Secretary of State a return order in the 1980 Hague Convention proceedings cannot be implemented. The two Conventions are not independent of each other but rather must operate hand in hand.

[127] ...there is no impediment to the High Court [the determining authority], in considering whether a defence under article 13(b) of the 1980 Hague Convention is made out, to making factual findings in relation to the constituent elements of the risk of refoulement. That is not cutting across or directly interfering in the exercise by the Secretary of State of her exclusive powers with respect to the control of immigration and asylum. The findings in the 1980 Hague Convention proceedings are clearly potentially relevant but

they do not discharge the Secretary of State from her statutory obligation to make her own independent assessment nor do they bind the Secretary of State.

[140] an application for asylum is pending and will not have been determined until the conclusion of the appeal process in accordance with section 104(1) of the 2002 Act.

[152] ...there cannot be an effective remedy under an in-country appeal process if in the meantime a child has in fact been returned under the 1980 Hague Convention to the country from which they have sought refuge. Accordingly, an in- country appeal acts as a bar to the implementation of a return order in 1980 Hague Convention proceedings. Due to the time taken by the in-country appeal process this bar is likely to have a devastating impact on 1980 Hague Convention proceedings. I would suggest that this impact should urgently be addressed by consideration being given as to a legislative solution.

[153] ... an out-of-country appeal would not act as a bar to the implementation of a return order in 1980 Hague Convention proceedings.

The Supreme Court in *G v G* also considered practical points and desirable steps to take in cases where the interplay between the two proceedings arise. These include, amongst others, recognising that it is the Secretary of State (not the family court) that has sole responsibility for both examining and determining claims for international protection; the Secretary of State should be requested to intervene in the 1980 Hague Convention proceedings; joining the child as a party to the proceedings; there being a specialist asylum team assigned to such cases; documents in the Convention proceedings should be made available to the Secretary of State, and consideration should be given, at the earliest opportunity, to disclosing the asylum documents into Convention proceedings.

See section 5.5 below for further discussions on human rights under Article 20 of the 1980 Hague Convention.

5.3.3 Evidence

From a practitioner's perspective, the gathering of evidence may include the use of police and medical reports, expert psychiatric or psychological reports in determining e.g., the 'grave risk of harm' to the child in domestic violence allegations. Directions in respect of expert evidence should comply with the provisions under FPR 2010 25. The evaluative exercise a court may conduct in dealing with disputed matters should be thorough, limited, and expeditious. Should oral evidence be deemed necessary, or the instruction of an expert, as in *Klentzeris v. Klentzeris* [2007] EWCA Civ 533 it should be focused on limited relevant issues. Where expert evidence is being contemplated, the HCCH Guide to Good Practice offers three focused questions: 1) does the court need an expert opinion? 2) for what specifically does the court need it? and, 3) who should the expert be?[87]

Oral evidence

As to oral witness evidence in general,[88] in *Re F (A Minor)*[89] Butler-Sloss, L.J. stated that the 'admission of oral evidence in Convention cases should be allowed sparingly'.[90] The same was noted in *Re K (Abduction: Child's Objections)*[91] where Wall J commented that 'the procedure under

---

[87] Hague Conference on Private International Law, 'Guide to Good Practice under the HCCH Convention of 25 October 1980 on the Civil Aspects of International Child Abduction – Part VI – Article 13(1)(b) March 2020 ('HCCH Guide to Good Practice on Article 13(1)b)'), para. 90.

[88] In relation to expert and non-expert witnesses.

[89] *Re F (A Minor)* [1995] Fam. 224 (C.A.) (Butler-Sloss, L.J.).

[90] ibid [553F].

[91] *Re K. (Abduction: Child's Objections)* [1995] 1 FLR 977, [1995] Fam Law 468.

the Convention is summary…to hear oral evidence on disputed issues of fact would defeat the essential purpose of the Convention…'.[92] The essence of these precedents remain true to this day. In practice, the English court uses its discretion to decide whether to hear 'limited' oral evidence from the parties if the court considers it necessary.[93] The leading UK Supreme Court dicta in *Re E (Children)* [2011] UKSC 27 stated that 'it will rarely be appropriate to hear oral evidence of the allegations under article 13(1) b)'[94] and therefore those allegations and their rebuttals are not usually cross examined.[95] This position was further reiterated in *Re S (a Child)*[96] when the Supreme Court overturned the Court of Appeal decision to order a return,[97] observing that one of the 'unfortunate features' of the judgment was the 'erroneous assumption' that the mother's allegations were entirely disputed and 'in the absence of oral evidence an assessment of their truth had lain beyond the judge's reach'.[98] In the previous case of *Re W (a child)*, Sedley LJ observed that it would be appropriate to hear oral evidence in an Article 13(1)*b)* case 'where the judge is satisfied that it is realistically capable of establishing the risk and degree in kind which the Article envisages'.[99]

---

[92] ibid [982].

[93] In addition, the tools used in ascertaining the degree of protection include the following process: 'information is sought from the requesting Central Authority, direct judicial communications are used, expert evidence on foreign law and practice is obtained, direct notice can be taken of foreign law' and 'information from one or the other (or both) of the parents' legal representatives in the requesting State can be provided.' Scotland echoes that information is also 'sought from the requesting Central Authority'. UK Response to Q5.2 (c) HCCH 2010 Questionnaire.

[94] *Re E (Children)* [32]; reiterated in *Re GP* [2017] EWHC 1480 (Fam) [14].

[95] ibid.

[96] *Re S (a Child)*.

[97] *S v C* [2011] EWCA Civ 1385.

[98] *Re S (a Child)* [7].

[99] *Re W (a child)* [2004] EWCA Civ 1366.

5.3.4 Protective Measures

Protective measures are mitigating or safeguarding measures used to reduce or ameliorate an identified risk of harm. As per the HCCH Guide to Good Practice on Article 13(1)*b)* these measures are often considered in cases where there is a grave risk of harm involving domestic violence or child abuse.[100] For example, measures analogous to a non-molestation order, occupation order, restraining order, non-harassment order, prohibition of access order, prohibited steps order and other orders aimed at protecting the child and parent whose welfare is at risk.

As case law has revealed, integral to determining whether a child would face a grave risk of harm if returned is considering protective measures and their ameliorative effects. It is important that practitioners are able to give thorough consideration to any protective measures offered, whether as the applicant or respondent. There is a fine line between generalised adequacy of protective measures and a competent examination of its efficacy against the facts of each individual case. The Perez-Vera Report reminds us that the exceptions were intended to be applied in a 'restrictive fashion'[101] and arguably, the English court is an exemplary jurisdiction in this regard, particularly in light of the approach to protective measures.

Before a non-return order is contemplated, the English courts will seek to first investigate whether adequate arrangements can be made to secure the protection of the child after his or her return; protection against the harm identified, whether physical, psychological, emotional, or other intolerable situation. According to paragraph 2.2(b) of the President's Guidance on Case Management and Mediation,[102] parties are expected

---

[100] HCCH Guide to Good Practice on Article 13(1)b), p. 34, para. 43.

[101] Perez-Vera Report, para 34.

[102] Practice Guidance on Case Management and Mediation of International Child Abduction Proceedings, Sir Andrew McFarlane LJ, published in

to turn their mind to the issue of protective measures as early on as possible. The President's Guide provides that:

> '(b) A direction pursuant to FPR 2010 r 12.46(a) for the expeditious filing of any further evidence to be relied on by the applicant in support of the application including, where it is not already contained in the evidence supporting the application, a description of any protective measures (including orders that may be subject to a declaration of enforceability or registration under Art 26 of the 1996 Hague Convention or, where appropriate, undertakings) the applicant is prepared, without prejudice to his or her case, to offer for the purpose of securing the child's return, including the extent to which any undertakings offered and accepted in this jurisdiction are capable of enforcement in the requesting jurisdiction.
>
> (c) A direction pursuant to FPR 2010 r 12.50(2)(a) for the filing and serving of the respondent's answer.
>
> (d) A direction pursuant to FPR 2010 r 12.50(1) for the filing of the respondent's evidence in support of the answer, to include the factual basis of the exceptions relied on (if any) and details of any protective measures the respondent seeks (including, where appropriate, undertakings and the extent to which any undertakings offered and accepted in this jurisdiction are capable of enforcement in the requesting jurisdiction) in the event that the court orders the child's return.'

Parties are invited to provide details of any protective measures offered or sought without prejudice to their case, but enabling the court to, in

March 2023 (hereafter 'President's Practice Guidance on Case Management and Mediation').

due course, consider the proposed protective measures once the alleged risk of harm is identified. This would also allow the court to pinpoint at an early stage whether a need for an expert arises out of any of the points raised on measures of protection. This is particularly so in non-Convention States where the safety net of the 1980 and 1996 Hague Convention is not available. A closer look at the national laws of the requesting State is necessary.

In reality, respondent parents may be reluctant to propose measures of protection and might instead mount a case arguing that they would not return and that a separation from the child would be e.g., intolerable. In this regard, practitioners would do well to examine the case on protective measures forensically – as they would all other aspects of the case – and determine how best to present their client's position. Courts are attuned to circumstances where parents may be unwilling (tactically) or unable to return for other reasons. The Guide to Good Practice on Article 13(1)*b)* reminds Contracting States that the focus of the grave risk analysis is the effect on the child (*Re A (Children) (Abduction: Article 13b)* [2021] EWCA Civ 939), and even where the high threshold of grave risk is met should separation occur, the courts are still minded to consider protective measures that could 'lift the obstacle to the taking parent's return'.[103] In the case of *C v B* [2019] EWHC 2593 (Fam) which concerned a mother's opposition to accompanying her three children back to Germany, in rejecting the mother's Article 13(1)*b)* defence based on separation, Peel QC J stated that 'plainly the abducting parent cannot avoid the provisions of the Hague Convention by a manipulated, contrived situation which purports to create a defence where there is none. Equally, the abducting parent cannot be deprived of relying upon a defence if his or her reaction is authentic and a direct consequence of the perceived risk upon return i.e., if it is a symptom of the circumstances giving rise to the defence.'[104] Further in *C v C (Abduction: Rights of Custody)* [1989] 1 FLR 403 [410D-F] Butler-Sloss LJ emphasised that the court needed to weigh

---

[103] Guide to Good Practice on Article 13(1)b), para. 65.

[104] *C v B* [2019] EWHC 2593 (Fam), [61].

up and balance respective factors, observing that 'I must place in the balance and as of the greatest importance the effect of the court refusing the application under the Convention because of the refusal of the mother to return for her own reasons, not for the sake of the child. Is a parent to create the psychological situation, and then rely upon it? If the grave risk of psychological harm to a child is to be inflicted by the conduct of the parent who abducted him, then it would be relied upon by every mother of a young child who removed him out of the jurisdiction and refused to return.'

Protective measures aimed at ameliorating the grave risks of harm may include orders akin to non-molestation orders, occupation orders, non-harassment orders and prohibitive steps orders. For example, in the Court of Appeal decision of *In the Matter of M (Children)* [2016] EWCA Civ 942 [8] which involved the return of children to the USA, the nature of protective measures proposed included to 'a.) not seek the mother's prosecution for child abduction; b.) not attend the airport of arrival; c.) to submit to a non-molestation order; d.) not remove the children from the mother's care; e.) to provide a three-bedroom property for the exclusive use of mother and children and pay the rent and outgoings; f.) to make other reasonable maintenance provision; and g.) to pay for the children's return flights. In this case, the issue was the effectiveness of such measures, with the Court of Appeal upholding the return order but directing that 'the father provides evidence [...] that a consent order has been entered into the Superior Court of New Jersey... and secondly that the landlord of his present accommodation consents to the subletting or assignment of the tenancy to the mother, or otherwise her exclusive occupation of the same.' [24].

Undertakings

We are probably well past the era of seeking to persuade a court of the inefficacy of undertakings, especially in cases where domestic abuse is in issue. But for completeness, Beaumont and McEleavy describe undertakings as 'promises offered, or in certain circumstances imposed upon an applicant to overcome obstacles which may stand in the way of returning a wrongfully removed or retained child'.[105] A practice that has arguably originated from our courts, it is now widely recognised that voluntary undertakings are hugely problematic[106] and are in fact unenforceable promises, which is particularly worrying in the context of domestic abuse. Professor Freeman's study has shown how 'one parent described how the left-behind parent referred to the undertakings he had been given to the English courts as 'toilet paper'[107] and another stated that he found that 'the police did not want to know'.[108] Thus, if undertakings were entertained in cross border child abduction proceedings, practitioners should be alive to the fact that they are largely ineffective and that the issue of enforceability should be addressed by seeking the terms of those promises under the auspices of the 1996 Hague Convention or incorporated into a separate mirror order. Having said that, in some instances, the court may lean towards undertakings having concluded that the domestic abuse alleged does not satisfy the Article 13(1)*b*) exception (see *AT v SS* [2015] EWHC 2703 (Fam)). The understanding or utility of undertakings may vary amongst jurisdictions that employ them within their domestic laws. From a practitioner's perspective, soft landing measures such as the payment of flight tickets may suffice as an undertaking especially when the effectiveness of those

---

[105] See Paul Beaumont and Peter McEleavy, *The Hague Convention on International Child Abduction* (Oxford University Press, Oxford 1999), p.158.

[106] See for example Schuz, 291-293: the use of undertakings has been subject to criticisms by both the abductor and the left-behind parent, 292; Roxanne Hoegger, 'What If She Leaves – Domestic Violence Cases Under the Hague Convention' (2013) 18(1) Berkeley Women's L.J. 181; Marilyn Freeman, 'International Child Abduction: Is It all Back to Normal Once the Child Returns Home?' (2011) International Family Law) (hereafter 'Freeman, Is it All Back to Normal'); Marilyn Freeman, 'Parental Child Abduction: The Long-Term Effects' (2014) International Centre for Family Law, Policy, and Practice [11]- [12], [14] and [17].

[107] Freeman, Is It All Back to Normal' [39].

[108] ibid, para. 40.

promises can be easily gauged (e.g., to facilitate a return order, there is a motivation to purchase flight tickets ahead of the (parent) and child's departure). However, practitioners, especially those for the left behind parent, should be prepared to scrutinise how concrete and adequate the measures are, in the interest of their client and the child. The ECtHR in *X v Latvia* emphasised that, as the preamble to the 1980 Hague Convention provides for children's return 'to the State of their habitual residence'[109,] the courts must satisfy themselves that adequate safeguards are convincingly provided in that country, and, in the event of a known risk, tangible and relevant protective measures are put in place.[110]

Soft landing measures

The HCCH Guide to Good Practice on Article 13(1)*b)* notes that there are circumstances where additional measures to assist the implementation of a return order may be necessitated (see *Re J (A Child) (Reunite International Abduction Centre and others intervening)* [2015] UKSC; [2015] 3 WLR 1827). Measures such as the applicant left-behind parent purchasing flight tickets, the provision of a home (or vacating the family home), payment of maintenance or a down payment for rent, or to obtain legal advice upon return to the country of habitual residence. There may of course be overlaps between soft-landing measures and protective measures, having said that, the HCCH Guide to Good Practice on Article 13(1)*b)* states that the Hague court cannot make orders that are not required to mitigate an established grave risk.[111]

---

[109] *X. v. Latvia*, para. 108.

[110] ibid.

[111] HCCH Guide to Good Practice on Article 13(1)b), p. 35.

5.3.5 The 1996 Hague Convention

The 1996 Hague Convention supports and supplements[112] the 1980 Hague Convention[113] by addressing the lacuna that exists in the latter in that there is no direct power under the Hague Convention to make protective orders.[114] A gap which *the Recast Regulation*, subsequent to the UK's exit from the EU and end of the transition period, has sought to bridge. In England & Wales, the recognition and enforcement of measures of protection made within child abduction proceedings (including undertakings) is now facilitated by the 1996 Hague Convention. Such measures should be treated as urgent measures of

---

[112] Thorpe LJ in *Re Y (A Child) (Abduction: Undertakings Given for Return of Child)* [2013] EWCA Civ 129 [9]. It is also said to have inspired some of the rules under Brussels II *bis*, such as Article 15: Thalia Kruger and Liselot Samyn, "Brussels II bis: Successes and Suggested Improvements" (2016) 12 Journal of Private International Law 132 at 150 discussing the interaction between Brussels II *bis* and the 1996 Convention.

[113] See Nigel Lowe, 'The Impact of the 1996 Convention on International Child Abduction', Division 5, Chapter 5, Clarke Hall & Morrison on Children (2017) (hereafter 'The Impact of the 1996 Convention'), 882: It is further stated that its 'clear purpose' is to 'secure the primacy' of the Hague Convention. See also Nigel Lowe, 'The Applicable Laws Provisions of the 1996 Hague Convention on the Protection of Children and the Impact of the Convention on International Child Abduction' (2010) International Family Law 51-58; Permanent Bureau of the Hague Conference, Practical Handbook on the operation of the Hague Convention of 19 October 1996 on Jurisdiction, Applicable Law, recognition, Enforcement and Co-operation in respect of Parental responsibility and Measures of the Protection of Child (2014).

[114] The Impact of the 1996 Convention, [902].

protection, with Article 11[115] as the jurisdictional basis, and Article 23[116] enabling recognition by operation of law in all other Contracting States. Although urgency is not defined, as articulated by Baroness Hale, it would be 'difficult to envisage'[117] a court not considering such an abduction case to be urgent pursuant to Article 11.

Articles 11 and 23-27 provide:

> (1) In all cases of urgency, the authorities of any Contracting State in whose territory the child or property belonging to the child is present have jurisdiction to take any necessary measures of protection.

> (2) The measures taken under the preceding paragraph with regard to a child habitually resident in a Contracting State shall lapse as soon as the authorities which have jurisdiction under Articles 5 to 10 have taken the measures required by the situation.

---

[115] Article 11 provides for jurisdiction as it states that "(1) In all cases of urgency, the authorities of any Contracting State in whose territory the child or property belonging to the child is present have jurisdiction to take any necessary measures of protection." See also POAM Best Practice Guide in Trimmings K, Dutta A, Honorati C and Zupan M (eds), *Domestic Violence and Parental Child Abduction* (1st edn, Intersentia 2022).

[116] *Re Y (A Child) (Abduction: Undertakings Given for Return of Child)* [2013] EWCA Civ 129. Following *Re Y*, authorities that have shown the High Court's utility of the 1996 Hague Convention, such as *RD v DB* [2015] EWHC 1817 (Fam), *In the matter of A (A Child) (Hague Abduction; Art 13(b): Protective Measures)* [2019] EWHC 649 (Fam) and *In the Matter of S O D*, High Court, 31 January 2019 (unreported).

[117] *Re J (A Child) (Reunite International Abduction Centre and others intervening)* [2015] UKSC; [2015] 3 WLR 1827, para. 39. See also Edward Devereux KC, '*Re J*: the 1996 Hague Convention in the Supreme Court' (2016) International Family Law, 21-24.

(3) The measures taken under paragraph 1 with regard to a child who is habitually resident in a non-Contracting State shall lapse in each Contracting State as soon as measures required by the situation and taken by the authorities of another State are recognised in the Contracting State in question.

Article 23

(1) The measures taken by the authorities of a Contracting State shall be recognised by operation of law in all other Contracting States.

(2) Recognition may however be refused -

a) if the measure was taken by an authority whose jurisdiction was not based on one of the grounds provided for in Chapter II;

b) if the measure was taken, except in a case of urgency, in the context of a judicial or administrative proceeding, without the child having been provided the opportunity to be heard, in violation of fundamental principles of procedure of the requested State;

c) on the request of any person claiming that the measure infringes his or her parental responsibility, if such measure was taken, except in a case of urgency, without such person having been given an opportunity to be heard;

d) if such recognition is manifestly contrary to public policy of the requested State, taking into account the best interests of the child;

e) if the measure is incompatible with a later measure taken in the non-Contracting State of the habitual residence of the child, where this later measure fulfils the requirements for recognition in the requested State;

f) if the procedure provided in Article 33 has not been complied with.

According to Article 24

Without prejudice to Article 23, paragraph 1, any interested person may request from the competent authorities of a Contracting State that they decide on the recognition or non-recognition of a measure taken in another Contracting State. The procedure is governed by the law of the requested State.

Article 25

The authority of the requested State is bound by the findings of fact on which the authority of the State where the measure was taken based its jurisdiction.

Article 26

(1) If measures taken in one Contracting State and enforceable there require enforcement in another Contracting State, they shall, upon request by an interested party, be declared enforceable or registered for the purpose of enforcement in that other State according to the procedure provided in the law of the latter State.

(2) Each Contracting State shall apply to the declaration of enforceability or registration a simple and rapid procedure.

(3) The declaration of enforceability or registration may be refused only for one of the reasons set out in Article 23, paragraph 2.

Article 27

> Without prejudice to such review as is necessary in the
> application of the preceding Articles, there shall be no review
> of the merits of the measure taken.

In the case of *B v B*[118] which involved the father's application for the
return of a girl, aged 9, to Lithuania. Mostyn J considered the mother's
defences under Article 13,[119] which included amongst others[120] that the
child would be exposed to an 'unacceptable or intolerable risk of
harm'.[121] In his judgment, His Lordship found that necessary measures
could be made in this case under Article 11 and that these can in turn be
recognised under Article 23 in all Contracting States to the 1996
Convention. The protective orders made pursuant to Article 11 included
prohibiting the father from molesting the mother, approaching within
100 metres of the mother's home, seeking an order for contact pending
resolution in the Lithuanian court and that the child shall remain in the
custody of the mother.[122] Mostyn J took the view that there would be
'no risk' under Article 13(1) *b)* as the measures would ensure a safeguard
against the same.

Where measures are taken under Article 23 of the 1996 Hague
Convention, and there is a doubt about whether such measures will be
recognised by operation of law in another Contracting State, steps should
also be taken by the left-behind parent to obtain recognition under
Article 24.[123] It is a provision governed by the law of the requested State.

---

[118] *B v B* [2014] EWHC 1804 (Fam).

The father had made admissions of violence in his statement.

[120] The child's objections under Article 13 (2) of the 1980 Hague
Convention.

[121] *B v B*, para.26.

[122] ibid, para.31.

[123] Permanent Bureau of the Hague Conference, Practical Handbook on the
operation of the Hague Convention of 19 October 1996 on Jurisdiction,

In circumstances where the court is satisfied that the measures are available, additional safeguards can be put in place by ensuring that Article 24 is utilised. It is envisaged that 'it is only at the time when the measure is invoked that a possible dispute over the existence of a ground for non-recognition may be the subject of a ruling'.[124] Therefore, the left-behind parent, regarded as an 'interested person', would be tasked with taking steps to remedy any such defect that may arise as to the recognition of the measures made under Article 23 of the 1996 Convention. In the case of *Re Y (A Child)*[125] an issue arose as to whether the Cypriot courts would recognise the undertakings made with the same effect and strength of a court order as deemed by the UK courts. To remedy this, and whilst the mother's appeal was pending in respect of the return order made by the trial judge, the father sought recognition of the order (including the undertakings) in Cyprus, and this was granted by the family court of Limassol.[126] The mother's appeal was subsequently dismissed.

Article 23 (1) of the 1996 Hague Convention sets out a rule of recognition whereby 'measures taken by the authorities of a Contracting State shall be recognised by operation of law in all other Contracting States'. However, pursuant to Article 23(2), such measures may be challenged on six grounds and recognition may be refused.[127] The term

---

Applicable Law, recognition, Enforcement and Co-operation in respect of Parental responsibility and Measures of the Protection of Child (2014), p.108-109 (hereafter '1996 Hague Convention, Practical Handbook'); and Paul Lagarde, 'Explanatory Report on the 1996 Hague Child Protection Convention' II (1998) 534-605. See also Emma Nash, 'Recognition under the 1996 Hague Convention' (2015), International Family Law, 264-269: reviewing Article 24 of the 1996 Convention.

[124] 1996 Hague Convention, Practical Handbook, para. 10.17.

[125] *Re Y (A Child) (Abduction: Undertakings Given for Return of Child)* [2013] EWCA Civ 129, [2013] 2.F.L.R. 649.

[126] An order for the 'registration and/or recognition and/or execution' of the order dated 3 December 2012.

[127] Article 23(2) provides an exhaustive list of the grounds on which recognition may be refused.

recognition 'by operation of law' means that the measures can be recognised in the requested State and have effect without the commencement of proceedings.[128] The measure to be recognised can be evidenced by way of written documentation or in urgent cases, by telephone[129] Once the enforceable measure is taken in one Contracting State, Article 26(1) provides that such a measure shall 'upon request by an interested party, be declared enforceable or registered for the purpose of enforcement in that other State according to the procedure provided in the law of the latter State'. From an English perspective, an incoming application for the recognition of a foreign order is dealt with under Part 31 of the Family Procedure Rules (Registration of Orders under the Hague Convention 1996). Part 31.4, which provides that:

> (1) Any interested person may apply to the court for an order that the judgment be registered, recognised or not recognised.

> (2) An application for registration, recognition or non-recognition must be–

> (a) made to a district judge of the principal registry; and

> (b) in the form and supported by the documents and the information required by a practice direction.

The circulation and thus enforcement of protective measures made in this jurisdiction requires registration or a declaration of enforceability in the State of habitual residence. In practice, however, this seems to be overlooked and it is assumed that where orders are made within Hague return proceedings combining the 1980 and the 1996 Hague Conventions, there is automatic recognition. Different jurisdictions operate Article 26 according to the *lex fori*, and this includes situations

---

[128] 1996 Hague Convention, Practical Handbook, p. 103.

[129] ibid.

where only the process of registration is possible, or only by an enforceability declaration or both. Further, Article 26(2) envisages that the procedure of declaration of enforceability and registration, which is governed by the law of the State of enforcement, must be 'simple and rapid'. However, it is also possible for such declaration to be refused on one of the grounds on which recognition can be denied pursuant to Article 23(2). Thereafter, Article 28 provides that once the measure has been declared enforceable or registered for enforcement, it has to be enforced as if it had been taken by the authorities of the State of enforcement. The actual enforcement takes place 'in accordance with the law of the requested State to the extent provided by such law, taking into consideration the best interests of the child.'[130]

In cases involving domestic violence, practitioners should be seeking water-tight and clearly prescribed protective measures such as terms akin to a non-molestation and occupation orders (but ensuring that the terminology reflects an equivalent measure of protection in the State of habitual residence). The measures should be incorporated into the return order or made in the form of specific requirements as a condition attached to the return and appended to the order. It is further proposed that where concerns persist (particularly in relation to Article 26(2)), advance recognition under Article 24 is an avenue to pursue. Another option is to make an application for an order mirroring the protective measures in the child abduction proceedings and for that order to be obtained from the State of habitual residence prior to return, such as in *Re Y (A Child)*. It is likely that the onus would rest on the left-behind parent. In non-Convention cases, it is generally expected that an expert report is obtained to set out the position on national law and the procedure on recognition and enforcement in the State of habitual residence.

---

[130] 1996 Hague Convention, Article 28.

5.4 The Objections of a Child under Article 13(2)

Article 13(2) provides that:

> 'The judicial or administrative authority may also refuse to
> order the return of the child if it finds that the child objects
> to being returned and has attained an age and degree of
> maturity at which it is appropriate to take account of its
> views.'

The Explanatory Report articulates that the Hague Convention 'provides
that the child's views concerning the essential question of its return or
retention may be conclusive...provided it has...attained an age and
degree of maturity...the Convention gives children the possibility of
interpreting their own interests'.[131]

The starting point is to consider whether the child has reached an age
and degree of maturity at which it is appropriate to take account of his
or her views. Thereafter a discretionary exercise is undertaken, with
regards to all the evidence (including professional opinion of CAFCASS)
on the weight to attach. The views of the child are not in themselves
determinative. In relation to taking account of a child's objections and
the meaning thereof, Baroness Hale made it clear that there was a
difference between 'taking account of' a child's views and acting in
accordance with those views, thereby resolving a previous debate in the
authorities about the meaning of the words 'take account of.' In *Re D*,
Baroness Hale stated that it would have been appropriate to have taken
account of this child's views at the date of the first instance hearing, when
he was aged seven and a half. She indicated that had the proceedings been
completed in August 2005 (when the child was only just aged seven) it
might well have been inappropriate to have canvassed his views. Once
the proceedings went on beyond that date, however, the child 'had

---

[131] Perez-Vera Report, para. 30.

reached an age where it could no longer be taken for granted that it was inappropriate for him to be given the opportunity of being heard.'[132]

As to discretion, *In Re M and another (Children) (Abduction: Rights of Custody)* [2007] UKHL 55,[133] Baroness Hale, stated at paragraph 46 that:

> '… Once the discretion comes into play, the court may have to consider the nature and strength of the child's objections, the extent to which they are "authentically her own" or the product of the influence of the abducting parent, the extent to which they coincide or are at odds with other considerations which are relevant to her welfare, as well as the general Convention considerations referred to earlier. The older the child, the greater the weight that her objections are likely to carry. But that is far from saying that the child's objections should only prevail in the most exceptional circumstances.'

In *Re T (Abduction: Child's Objections to Return)*[134] Ward LJ noted some considerations that the court should find relevant and take into account in exercising discretion. The Court of Appeal case of *Re J (Abduction: Child's Objections to Return)*[135] cited and upheld Ward LJ's guidance that:

> (a) The child's own perspective of what is in the interests, short, medium, and long term.

---

[132] *Re D (A Child)*, para. 64.

[133] Hereafter 'Re M and another', also known as *Re M (Abduction: Zimbabwe)* [2007] UKHL 55, [2008] 1 AC 1288.

[134] [2000] 2 FLR 192 Ward LJ, p. 204.

[135] [2004] EWCA Civ 428, [2004] 2 FLR 64.

(b) The extent to which the reasons for objection are rooted in reality or might reasonably appear to the child to be so grounded.

(c) The extent to which the views have been shaped or even coloured by undue influence and pressure, directly or indirectly exerted by the abducting parent.

(d) The extent to which the objections will be mollified on return and, where it is the case, on removal from any pernicious influence from the abducting parent?

In *Re J & K (Abduction: Objections of Child)* [2005] 1 FLR 273 Wilson J considered the apparent difference of views expressed in the Court of Appeal and described it as being in reality a difference of emphasis. The court at the discretionary stage will be seeking to weigh up and balance the age and degree of maturity of the child and the nature and strength of those objections.

In *Re G (Children)* [2010] EWCA Civ 1232 the decision to summarily return two children, aged 13 and 9, to Canada was overturned by the Court of Appeal. Although the mother pleaded the defences of Article 13(a) acquiescence, Article 13(1)*b)* grave risk and Article 13(2) child's objections, the proceedings focused on Article 13(2). The Court of Appeal held that the first instance decision was correct on the evidence before it but overturned the decision on the basis of fresh evidence. The fresh evidence consisted of two statements from the 13-year old child, and a meeting the court conducted with the child. The meeting between the court and child was a highly unusual step. Indeed, it was the first time that Thorpe LJ had ever conducted such a meeting. However, he took the view that such a step was justified and necessary in the case. It is important to draw attention to the fact that the first instance judge did not meet the child. Further, in *Re W (abduction: child's objections)* [2010] EWCA Civ 520 Wilson LJ at paragraph 24 observed that taking into account a child's objectives '...means no more than what it says so, albeit bounded of course by considerations of age and degree of maturity, it represents a fairly low threshold requirement. In particular it does not follow that the court should 'take account' of a child's objections only if they are so solidly based that they are likely to be determinative of the discretionary exercise which is to follow.' *In Re M and another (Children) (Abduction: Rights of Custody)* [2007] UKHL 55 where discretion is concerned, the court 'is entitled to take into account the various aspects of the Convention policy, alongside the circumstances which gave the court a discretion in the first place and the wider considerations of the child's rights and welfare' [43]. At [46], Lady Hale noted that 'in child's objections cases, the range of considerations may be even wider than those in the other exceptions. The exception itself is brought into play when only two conditions are met: first, that the child herself objects to being returned and secondly, that she has attained an age and degree of maturity at which it is appropriate to take account of her views.'

Established case law in this area is anchored by the Court of Appeal authorities: *Re F (children) (wrongful retention: child's objections)* [2016] 1 FCR 168 and *Re M and others (Children) (Abduction: Child's Objections)* [2016] Fam. In *Re F*, Black LJ reiterated that the question a judge must ask is *'Does the child object to being returned to his or her country of habitual residence?'* and that the 'over-prescriptive or over-intellectualised' approach is to be discouraged, summarising as follows:

> '69. In the light of all of this, the position should now be, in my view, that the gateway stage is confined to a straightforward and fairly robust examination of whether the simple terms of the Convention are satisfied in that the child objects to being returned and has attained an age and degree of maturity at which it is appropriate to take account of his or her views. Sub-tests and technicality of all sorts should be avoided. In particular, the Re T approach to the gateway stage should be abandoned.
>
> 76. I now turn to how the law will work in practice. I do not intend to say a great deal on this score. The judges who try

these cases do so regularly and build up huge experience in dealing with them, as do the CAFCASS officers who interview the children involved. I do not think that they need (or will be assisted by) an analysis of how to go about this part of their task. In making his or her findings and evaluation, the judge will be able to draw upon the entirety of the material that has been assembled in relation to the child's objections exception and to pick from it those features which are relevant to his or her determination. The starting point is the wording of Article 13 which requires, as the authorities which I would choose to follow confirm, a determination of whether the child objects, whether he or she has attained an age and degree of maturity at which it is appropriate to take account of his or her views, and what order should be made in all the circumstances. What is relevant to each of these decisions will vary from case to case.

77. I am hesitant about saying more lest what I say should be turned into a new test or taken as some sort of compulsory checklist. I hope that it is abundantly clear that I do not intend this and that I discourage an over-prescriptive or over-intellectualised approach to what, if it is to work with proper despatch, has got to be a straightforward and robust process. I risk the following few examples of how things may play out at the gateway stage, trusting that they will be taken as just that, examples offered to illustrate possible practical applications of the principles. So, one can envisage a situation, for example, where it is apparent that the child is merely parroting the views of a parent and does not personally object at all; in such a case, a relevant objection will not be established. Sometimes, for instance because of age or stage of development, the child will have nowhere near the sort of understanding that would be looked for before reaching a conclusion that the child has a degree of maturity at which it is appropriate to take account of his or her views.

Sometimes, the objection may not be an objection to the right thing. Sometimes, it may not be an objection at all, but rather a wish or a preference.'

5.4.1 The Child's Age

The 1980 Hague Convention does not stipulate a minimum age at which a child's objections or views can be taken into account. In *Re T (Abduction: Child's Objections to Return)* the court took into account the views of the child who was aged 7 ½ even though the CAFCASS officer was of the opinion that the child's objection was influenced by the mother. In *Re R (Abduction: Acquiescence)* [1995] 1 FLR 716 the majority of the Court of Appeal (Millett LJ dissenting on this point) held that it was appropriate to 'take account of the views of two children aged 7 ½ and 6, although they went on to override those views and order their return. In *B v K* [1993] 1 FCR 382 Johnson J took account of the objections of two boys aged 9 and 7, their views were upheld. In *Re J & K (Abduction: Objections of Child)* [2005] 1 FLR 273] however, Wilson J held in respect of a 9-year old child of normal intelligence that he had 'only just' attained an age and degree of maturity at which it was appropriate for the court to take account of his views. Since the case of *Re D (A Child)*, the English court's approach appears to centre around the age of 7, though in reality, the age of a child is just one part of the consideration.

5.4.2 The Child's Maturity

Where the maturity of the child is in question, Ward LJ in *Re T (Abduction: Child's Objections to Return)* [2000] 2 FLR 192 cited and approved the findings of Waite LJ in *Re S (Minors) (Abduction: Acquiescence)* [1994] 1 FLR 819 stating that:

'When Article 13 speaks of an age and maturity level at which it is appropriate to take account *of a child's views, the inquiry which it envisages is not restricted to a generalised appraisal of the child's capacity to form and express views which bear the hallmark of maturity. It is permissible (and indeed will often be necessary) for the court to make specific inquiry as to whether the child has reached a stage of development at which, when asked the question "Do you object to a return to your home country?" he or she can be relied on to give an answer which does not depend upon instinct alone, but is influenced by the discernment which a mature child brings to the question's implications for his or her own best interests in the long and short term.'*

Ward LJ further noted that a child 'may be mature enough for it to be appropriate for his views to be taken into account even though he may not have gained that level of maturity that she is fully emancipated from parental dependence and can claim autonomy of decision-making'.

5.4.3 Siblings

A possible difficulty arises where only one of two or more children is mature or old enough for his or her view to be taken into account. In *Re HB (Abduction: Children's Objections)*[136] Baroness Hale found that the objections of the younger child were insufficient to justify refusing to make an order for her return. The objections of the older child were more compelling. Nevertheless, Baroness Hale made an order for the return of both siblings in the exercise of her discretion so as to avoid splitting them up. A year later in 1998, the case was heard in the Court of Appeal[137] whereby the older child had returned to Denmark, but the younger child had refused to board the aeroplane. The Court of Appeal allowed the appeal on the basis that one year had elapsed in which the mother had done nothing to enforce the order. They commented, however, that Baroness Hale had been correct in her approach. A similar approach was taken in *Re T (Abduction: Child's Objections to Return)*[138]. It illustrates

---

[136] *Re (Abduction: Children's Objections)* [1997] 1 FLR 392.

[137] [1998] 1 FLR 422.

[138] [2000] 2 FLR 192.

the court's exercise of discretion and careful consideration of each individual child rather than considering them collectively.

In contrast, *TB v JB (Abduction: Grave Risk of Harm)*,[139] was a case in which the Court had to consider the objections of a 14-year old girl to return to New Zealand. She had three siblings: a 12-year old boy who had expressed a positive wish to return, and two younger children who were not old enough for their views to be considered by the court. The majority of the Court of Appeal decided that the 14-year old girl should be ordered to return, citing with approval the approach adopted by Baroness Hale in *Re HB (Abduction: Children's Objections)*.

In *Re J (Abduction: Child's Objections to Return)*[140] the Court of Appeal allowed an appeal against an order for the return to Croatia of two children aged (at the date of the judgments) 12 and 9. Their decision was based entirely upon the objections of the older child. The position of the younger child was not considered separately, as it appears to have been accepted that he should not be returned without his brother.

The overall trend of the authorities is that the courts are reluctant to make orders which fly in the face of strongly held and rational objections expressed by children who are old enough and mature enough to consider the consequences of their decision. However, the threshold appears high.

5.4.4 Participation of the Child

In *Re D (A Child)*, Lady Hale observed that 'children should be heard far more frequently in Hague Convention cases than has been the practice hitherto' (paragraph 59) …. because it 'is plainly not good enough to say that the abducting parent, with whom the child is living, can present the child's views to the court.'

---

[139] [2001] 2 FLR 515.

[140] [2004] EWCA Civ 428.

As per the President's Practice Guidance on Case Management and Mediation, the participation of the child must be considered at the first hearing, to include exploring the question whether an opportunity should be given to the child to be heard in proceedings. In doing so, the court will have regard to the age and maturity of the child (commonly referred to as the 'gateway stage'). In England and Wales, a child may be heard via an Officer of the CAFCASS High Court Team and/or through party status (separate representation). See also the HCCH Guide to Good Practice on Article 13(1)*b)* on the participation of the child in proceedings (para. 86)

5.4.5 Joinder

Where an application is made for the child as the subject of proceedings to be joined as a party, the starting point for practitioners are the provisions contained in FPR Part 16 (and Practice Direction 16A (Representation of Children)) which sets out the rules for the representation of children and the commission of reports in proceedings that involve children. In particular, the appointment of a children's guardian and the ambit of their duties is contained under Rule 16.3. PD16A, 7.4 provides that:

> When a child is made a party and a children's guardian is to be appointed –
>
> (a) consideration should first be given to appointing an officer of the Service or Welsh family proceedings officer. Before appointing an officer, the court will cause preliminary enquiries to be made of Cafcass or CAFCASS CYMRU. For the relevant procedure, reference should be made to the practice note issued by Cafcass in June 2006 and any modifications of that practice note.
>
> (b) If Cafcass or CAFCASS CYMRU is unable to provide a children's guardian without delay, or if for some other reason the appointment of an officer of the Service of Welsh family

proceedings officer is not appropriate, rule 16.24 makes further provision for the appointment of a children's guardian.

In determining whether the child should be joined as a party to proceedings and afforded separate representation, the court will consider whether it is in the child's best interest (FPR 16.2(1)). Williams J in *Re Q & V (1980 Hague Convention and inherent Jurisdiction Summary Return)* [2019] EWHC 490 (Fam) went further to state that 'in determining whether it is in a young person's best interests to be joined to proceedings the court must take account of issues relating to the autonomy of the young person and their own desire to participate. The court must also take into account matters such as the need for them to have a separate voice in order to ensure that their position is adequately advocated or understood. The court must weigh the impact of separate representation on their welfare and the potential negative impact of them being drawn into the parental conflict and the court arena but also positives in relation to what they might bring to the process and how it might ensure they bought into the outcome. Lastly the court must also consider the impact on the proceedings in terms of delay or expense.'

CAFCASS officers are also under the duty to advise the court if the best interests of a child are best protected by joining that child as a party to the proceedings. A Guardian ad Litem is then appointed (e.g., case of *RS v KS (Abduction: Wrongful Retention* [2009] 2 FLR 1231).

5.5 The Human Rights Exception: Article 20

Article 20 limits the return obligation of Article 12. It states that 'the return of the child under the provisions of Article 12 may be refused if this would not be permitted by the fundamental principles of the requested State relating to the protection of human rights and fundamental freedoms'. Article 20 sets down grounds in which a return may be denied. The summary point to draw from this is that the courts are afforded a further route through which a child's welfare and interests are weighed and protected. As per Beaumont and McEleavy Article 20 would not only apply to the child but to the custodial parent.[141] In essence, the focus on a child as per Convention objectives does not preclude the position of the taking parent. Unlike the other exceptions, the provision under Article 20 of the Hague Convention was not expressly incorporated into the 1985 Child Abduction and Custody Act. Before that, this Article was not applicable in the United Kingdom. However, through the adoption of the Human Rights Act 1988 ('HRA") which came into force in October 2000, Article 6[142] of the HRA gives effect to and thus, makes it unlawful for a court to act in a way that is incompatible with a person's right under the European Convention on Human Rights 1950, see *Re D (A Child)* [2006] [UKHL] 51 and subsequently *FE v YE* [2017] EWHC 2165 (Fam).

Of note, Article 20 is more than just a public policy clause, it acknowledges that a refusal to return on human rights grounds is possible, based on the internal laws of the State of refuge. In England and Wales, this may be the 1998 Human Rights Act which gives effect to the rights and freedoms guaranteed under the ECHR, or indeed the body of international human rights laws created under the auspices of the United Nations,[143] including the 1989 Convention on the Rights of the Child; or treaties that overlap with immigration laws such as the Convention

---

[141] See Paul Beaumont and Peter McEleavy, The Hague Convention on International Child Abduction (Oxford University Press, Oxford 1999) 174-175.

[142] Article 6 HRA: the right to a fair trial.

[143] Such as the 1948 Convention on the Prevention and Punishment of the Crime of Genocide, the 1965 International Convention on the Elimination of All Forms of Racial Discrimination, the 1979 Convention on the Elimination of All Forms of Discrimination against Women, the 1989 Convention on the Rights of the Child, and the 2006 Convention on the rights of Persons with Disabilities.

and Protocol relating to the Status of Refugees adopted on 25 July 1951 and 16 December 1976 ('the 1951 Geneva Convention').

In reality, Article 20 of the Convention is rarely utilised. The most recent HCCH statistical analysis showed that a non-return order was made only in two cases on the sole or combined basis of Article 20. None of these cases were decided in the English jurisdiction.[144] Like the other exceptions to return, Article 20 should be approached in a restrictive fashion. The Pérez-Vera report notes the 'exceptional nature' of the provision's application.[145] As such, invoking general human rights argument based on Article 6 of the ECHR (right to fair hearing)[146] or Article 8 of the ECHR (right to private and family life) does not compel an Article 20 case. The expectation is that these considerations are naturally examined in 1980 Hague cases. In fact, neighbouring EU member states of the Convention now have the benefit of the Recast Regulation,[147] which explicitly states that consideration of the best

---

[144] Nigel Lowe and Victoria Stephens, 'A statistical analysis of applications made in 2015 under the Hague Convention of 25 October 1980 on the Civil Aspects of International Child Abduction, Part I, Global Report' (September 2017); Part II – Regional Report (September 2017); and Part III – National Reports (July 2018). According to the Global report, the sole and multiple reasons for refusal based on Article 20 was 2 cases out of a total of 185 (see Annex 5 and 6). According to the regional report, refusal in 'regulation' cases amount to 1 case (and 1%), with 0% in non-regulation cases. Available at <https://www.hcch.net/en/publications-and-studies/details4/?pid=6598&dtid=32> accessed 20 June 2023.

[145] Elisa Perez-Vera, Explanatory Report on the 1980 Hague Child Abduction Convention, Acts and Documents of the Fourteenth Session (1980), 3 Child Abduction 426-476, 431, p.461

[146] See for example, Re M (Children) (Abduction: Rights of Custody) [2007] UKHL 55, Re K (Abduction: Psychological harm) [1995] 2 FLR 550 (of note, in Re K Article 20 had not yet been enacted into English domestic law until the 1998 Human Rights Act came into force in 2000).

[147] Council Regulation (EU) 2019/1111 of 25 June 2019 on jurisdiction, the recognition and enforcement of decisions in matrimonial matters and the

interests of the child shall be influenced by Article 24 of the Charter of Fundamental Rights of the European Union and the UNCRC.

Further, in the Convention's Explanatory Report, Professor Pérez-Vera makes the point that the provision requires the need to not only demonstrate the contradiction between the Hague Convention objectives and internal laws of the State of refuge, but to also show that the return would be prohibited because of protective principles of human rights.[148] Thus, the protection of such rights may be engaged when the taking parent is faced with persecution on the basis of race, religion, political stance, nationality, membership of a particular group, or threats to human rights as a result of war or other unsettled environment. In this regard, recent jurisprudence has examined the interplay between Hague Convention proceedings and immigration law, in particular, the relationship between the 1980 Hague Convention and the 1951 Geneva Convention.

In pursuing the Article 20 exception to return on the basis of threats to human rights and fundamental freedoms, *FE v YE* [2017] EWHC 2165 (Fam) and subsequently the Supreme court in *G v G (international child abduction)* [2021] UKSC 9 have confirmed that a grant of asylum / refugee status is a bar to a return order being made under the 1980 Hague Convention. Hague Convention cases produce orders of a procedural nature, whereas the grant of relief under the 1951 Geneva Convention is of a substantive nature. The grant of asylum to a taking parent and dependant child enshrouds their rights in protection from refoulement. As per Article 33 of the Geneva Convention *"[n]o Contracting State shall expel or return ("refouler") a refugee in any manner whatsoever to the frontiers of territories where his life or freedom would be threatened on*

---

matters of parental responsibility, and on international child abduction (hereafter "the Recast Regulation"). preamble, para. 19.

[148] Elisa Perez-Vera, Explanatory Report on the 1980 Hague Child Abduction Convention, Acts and Documents of the Fourteenth Session (1980), 3 Child Abduction 426-476, 431, p. 433.

account of his race, religion, nationality, member- ship of a particular social group or political opinion." In circumstances were asylum claims are pending, Appendix two attached to the *G v G* Supreme court judgment provides guidance on standard directions with suggestions to address problem areas such as the need for coordination with the Secretary of state and the need for expedition of any asylum appeal or judicial review.[149] Nevertheless, it is noteworthy than unlike the English courts' stance that a return order would breach the principle of non-refoulement where asylum application is pending or has been granted, initially other jurisdictions such as the US and Canadian courts have held the view that the grant of asylum is not determinative.[150] This position was rejected by Mostyn J in *FE v YE*.[151]

Finally, it is of note that often human rights arguments appear to underpin pleadings relating to the grave risk of harm (Article 13(1)*b*)) or the child's objections (Article 20). Indeed, the Guide to Good Practice acknowledges that risks such as political, economic or security situations in the State of habitual residence may fall under asserted grave risks of harm.[152] As such, reliance on Article 20 is comparatively scant. When

---

[149] *G v G (international child abduction)* [2021] UKSC 9, Appendix Two, p. 64-65.

[150] See for example, the Canadian decision of Court of Appeal (Ontario) in *AMRI v KER* [2011] ONCA 417 and the US Court of Appeal (first circuit) in the decision of *Sanchez v RGL* (2015) 761. F.3d 495. However, see more recent Canadian decision in the case on M.A.A v D.E.M.E (ONCA) on July 29, 2020, where the Ontario Court of Appeal found that family courts cannot issue return orders for children if their applications for asylum are still pending.

[151] *FE v YE* [2017] EWHC 2165 (Fam), paras. 22-24.

[152] Hague Conference on Private International Law, 'Guide to Good Practice under the HCCH Convention of 25 October 1980 on the Civil Aspects of International Child Abduction – Part VI – Article 13(1)(b)', 2020 (hereafter: 'HCCH Guide') para 61, available at https://assets.hcch.net/docs/225b44d3-5c6b-4a14-8f5b-57cb370c497f.pdf.

consideration was given to the ambit of Article 20, in both the Court of Appeal[153] and Supreme Court[154] in *G v G (international child abduction)* [2021] UKSC 9 it was held that the broad scope of Article 13(1)*b)* amply covers the position of a parent fleeing domestic violence. However, arguably, in cases of domestic violence, there is much to be said about exceptional but real circumstances where a victim or survivor of domestic violence asserts that a well-founded fear of persecution exists. This is because of the fear of abuse from the left behind parent for which adequate protection is not possible in the State of habitual residence. In other jurisdictions, courts have observed situations where perpetual disobedience and violation of orders[155] meant that the State of habitual residence was incapable (or unwilling) to protect the parent and therefore the child.[156] To that effect, one may formulate an argument that domestic violence is a form of persecution[157] pursuant to the 1951 Refugee Convention, and women, as a particular social group within the meaning of Article 1A of the Refugee Convention are entitled to seek refuge, having fled a country that is unable to protect them and their children.[158] Thus relying on the principle of non-refoulement. Where

---

[153] *In the matter of G (A Child) (Child Abduction)* [2020] EWCA Civ 1185, para. 41.

[154] *G v G (international child abduction)* [2021] UKSC 9, para. 155.

[155] See also the English decision in *LS v AS* [2014] EWHC 1626 (Fam).

[156] US case of Walsh v Walsh 221 F.3d 204, 221 (1st Cir. 2000), State Central Authority, Secretary to the Department of Human Services v Mander, No. (P) MLF1179 of 2003, p. 25 (INCADAT database), *Friedrich v Friedrich* (Friedrich II) 78 F.3d 1060, 1069 (6th Cir. 1996).

[157] Establishing a well-founded fear based on a subjective and objective element: SN & HM and 3 Dependants (Divorced Women – Risk on Return) Pakistan v. Secretary of State for the Home Department, CG [2004] UKIAT 00283, para. 34.

[158] Or other country where life is threatened: The Refugee Convention, 1951, The Travaux Preparatoires Analysed with a Commentary by Paul Weis <https://www.unhcr.org/uk/media/refugee-convention-1951-travaux-preparatoires-analysed-commentary-dr-paul-weis> accessed 20 June 2023.

internal laws are concerned, under the Human Rights Act, at the least, Articles 2[159] and 3 are engaged.

5.6 Setting Aside a Return or Non-Order

The legal framework can be found under FPR 12.52A, which provides that an application to set aside a return order, where there is no error of the court (in which case the appeal route should be pursued) shall be made under this rule. Where a return or non-return order is being challenged, PD12F deals with 'rare' circumstances where the court might set aside its own order on the basis that new information had come to light which 'fundamentally changes the basis on which the order was made'. Such an application will be met by a high threshold and will require supporting evidence. The reasons may be as follows [4.1A]:

> If the return order or non-return order was made under the 1980 Hague Convention, the court might set aside its decision where there has been fraud, material non-disclosure or mistake (which all essentially mean that there was information that the court needed to know in order to make its decision, but was not told), or where there has been a fundamental change in circumstances which undermines the basis on which the order was made. If you have evidence of such circumstances and wish to apply to the court to set aside its decision, you should use the procedure in Part 18 of the Rules.

> If the return order or non-return order was made under the inherent jurisdiction (see Part 3 of this Practice Direction), the court might set aside its decision for similar reasons as with return-non-return orders under the 1980 Hague

---

[159] Article 2 HRA: the right to be protected by law; Article 3 HRA: prohibition of torture.

Convention, but it also might set aside its decision because the welfare of the child or children requires it. If you have evidence of such circumstances and wish to apply to the court to set aside its decision, you should use the procedure in Part 18 of the Rules.

Any such application should be made promptly, and the court will also aim to deal with the application as expeditiously as possible.

See also, for example, the case of *Re W (Abductions: setting aside return order)* [2019] 1 FLR 400, Moylan LJ, *Re B (A Child)* [2021] 1 WLR 517 and *Re A (A Child) (1980 Hague Convention: Set Aside)* [2021] EWCA Civ 194. In Re B, the process following an application to set aside an order, reiterated in Re A (A Child) was suggested as follows '(a) the court will first decide whether to permit any reconsideration; (b) if it does, it will decide the extent of any further evidence; (c) the court will next decide whether to set aside the existing order; (d) if the order is set aside, the court will redetermine the substantive application'.

CHAPTER SIX

THE INHERENT JURISDICTION OF THE HIGH COURT

When a child is taken to or from a State that is not party to the Hague Convention, as can be seen from Figures 2.1 and 2.2 above, although the Hague Convention does not apply, however, there are alternative methods of seeking the return of the child. A parent may apply under the inherent jurisdiction of the High Court for a child taken to England to be returned to the non-Convention State; or an application for a child taken *out* of the jurisdiction to be returned to England and Wales. The latter in particular would often include an application to the court for the child to be made a Ward of the court, alongside other injunctive reliefs and/or remedies such as a (Tipstaff) passport orders, a Prohibited Steps Order, a Location Order, a Port Alert, Freezing Injunctions, and any other specific injunctive provisions. Making a child a Ward of the court is a protective measure in its own right, it is considered as part of inherent jurisdiction proceedings, vesting custody of the child in the court. On the issue of measures of protection, it is perhaps worth mentioning here that where the 1996 Hague Convention applies,[160] the court will not exercise its inherent jurisdiction (see *Re I-L (children) (1996 Hague Child Protection Convention: inherent jurisdiction)* [2019] EWCA Civ 1956).

When international parental child abduction cases are pursued under the inherent jurisdiction of the High Court, the court's paramount consideration is the child's welfare (a contrast to the nature of Hague proceedings). Notwithstanding this, it is noteworthy that a similar timeframe to Hague Convention cases is expected of non-Convention

---

[160] Or in some instances, the Family Law Act 1986.

cases, that being six weeks unless exceptional circumstances arise. The application for the summary return of a child under the inherent jurisdiction will be guided by the legal principles set out by Baroness Hale in the House of Lords decision of *Re J (A Child) (Custody Rights: Jurisdiction)* [2005] UKHL 40 (as between the Kingdom of Saudi Arabia and the UK) which were reiterated in *S v S* [2014] EWHC 575 (Fam) [21] (as between Bermuda and the UK). As per the Court of Appeal in *Re A and B (Children) (Summary return: Non-Convention State)* [2022] EWCA Civ 1664) it is a *summary welfare determination* that is envisaged. In principle, this may be an exercise that is swift, or one that is more detailed, much will depend on the facts of the case (including whether other factors such as PD12J is engaged). Nevertheless, in undertaking a summary welfare determination, the court shall give consideration to the welfare of each child as per section 1(1) of the Children Act 1989. However, unlike the welfare exercise under private or public law children proceedings, the court has a number of matters to contend with. The approach to the welfare analysis is not strictly relegated to the terms under the 1989 Children Act and an inquiry into all aspects of a child's welfare may not be necessary.

Re J (A Child) (Custody Rights: Jurisdiction) [2005] UKHL 40 reflects Baroness Hale's guidance on the court's approach to dealing with an application for a return order based on a summary welfare determination:

> 25. Hence, in all non-Convention cases, the courts have consistently held that they must act in accordance with the welfare of the individual child. If they do decide to return the child, that is because it is in his best interests to do so, not because the welfare principle has been superseded by some other consideration. This was so, even in those cases decided around the time that the Hague Convention was being implemented here, where it was held that the courts should take account of its philosophy: see, for example, *G v G (Minors) (Abduction)* [1991] 2 FLR 506. The Court of Appeal, in *Re P (A Minor) (Child Abduction: Non Convention*

Country) [1997] Fam 45 has held that the Hague Convention concepts are not to be applied in a non-Convention case. Hence, the first two propositions set out by Mr Justice Hughes in this case were entirely correct: the child's welfare is paramount, and the specialist rules and concepts of the Hague Convention are not to be applied by analogy in a non-Convention case.

26. Thirdly, however, the court does have power, in accordance with the welfare principle, to order the immediate return of a child to a foreign jurisdiction without conducting a full investigation of the merits. In a series of cases during the 1960s, these came to be known as 'kidnapping' cases. The principles were summed up by Lord Justice Buckley in *Re L (Minors) (Wardship: Jurisdiction)* [1974] 1 WLR 250, at p 264, rightly described by Lord Justice Ward in Re P and Re JA as the locus classicus:

> "To take a child from his native land, to remove him to another country where, maybe, his native tongue is not spoken, to divorce him from the social customs and contacts to which he has been accustomed, to interrupt his education in his native land and subject him to a foreign system of education, are all acts (offered here as examples and of course not as a complete catalogue of possible relevant factors) which are likely to be psychologically disturbing to the child, particularly at a time when his family life is also disrupted. If such a case is promptly brought to the attention of a court in this country, the judge may feel that it is in the best interests of the infant that these disturbing factors should be eliminated from his life as speedily as possible. A full investigation of the merits of the case in an English court may be incompatible with achieving this. The judge may well be persuaded

that it would be better for the child that those merits should be investigated in a court in his native country."

27. He went on to emphasise that in doing so, the court was not punishing the parent for her conduct but applying the cardinal rule. The same point was made by Lord Justice Ormrod in *Re R (Minors) (Wardship: Jurisdiction)* (1981) 2 FLR 416, at p 425: the 'so-called kidnapping' of the child, or the order of a foreign court, were relevant considerations,

'but the weight to be given to either of them must be measured in terms of the interests of the child, not in terms of penalising the 'kidnapper', or of comity, or any other abstraction. 'Kidnapping', like other kinds of unilateral action in relation to children, is to be strongly discouraged, but the discouragement must take the form of *a swift, realistic, and unsentimental assessment of the best interests of the child, leading, in proper cases, to the prompt return of the child to his or her own country*, but *not* the sacrifice of the child's welfare to some other principle of law.'

28. It is plain, therefore, that there is always a choice to be made. Summary return should not be the automatic reaction to any and every unauthorised taking or keeping a child from his home country. On the other hand, summary return may very well be in the best interests of the individual child.

See also *S v S* [2014] EWHC 575, *Re NY (A Child) (Reunite International and others intervening)* [2020] AC 665 and *Re A and B (Children) (Summary Return: Non-Convention State)* [2022] EWCA Civ 1664. For example, in *Re NY (A Child)* [at para. 48], Lord Wilson reiterated that in non-Convention cases, 'the court will initially examine whether the child's welfare requires it to conduct the extensive inquiry into certain matters which it would ordinarily conduct. Again, however, it would be wrong for that initial decision to be reached in a significantly different way in each of them.'

Given the ambit of the welfare enquiry, and in considering all relevant factors including any safeguarding concerns, Practice Direction 12J may be engaged, and so practitioners should be aware of this intersectionality. The courts will be considering the requirements under the Practice Direction and whether an enquiry into the allegations is required in order to properly address the welfare of the child.

In particular, PD 12J (FPR 2010) paragraphs 35 – 37 and 40 provide:

> [35] When deciding the issue of child arrangements, the court shall ensure that any order for contact will be safe and in the best interests of the child.
>
> [36] In the light of any findings of fact the court should apply the individual matters in the welfare checklist with reference to those findings; in particular, where relevant findings of domestic violence or abuse have been made, the court should in every case consider any harm which the child and the parent with whom the child is living has suffered as a consequence of that violence or abuse, and any harm which the child and the parent with whom the child is living, is at risk of suffering if a child arrangements order is made. The court should only make an order for contact if it can be satisfied that the physical and emotional safety of the child and the parent with whom the child is living can, as far as possible, be secured before during and after contact, and that the parent with whom the child is living will not be subjected to further controlling or coercive behaviour by the other parent.
>
> [37] In every case where a finding of domestic violence or abuse is made, the court should consider the conduct of both

parents towards each other and towards the child; in
particular, the court should consider –

a) the effect of the domestic violence or abuse on the child
    and on the arrangements for where the child is living;

b) the effect of the domestic violence or abuse on the child
    and its effect on the child's relationship with the
    parents;

c) whether the applicant parent is motivated by a desire
    to promote the best interests of the child or is using the
    process to continue a process of violence, abuse,
    intimidation, or harassment or controlling or coercive
    behaviour against the other parent;

d) the likely behaviour during contact of the parent
    against whom findings are made and its effect on the
    child; and

e) the capacity of the parents to appreciate the effect of
    past violence or abuse and the potential for future
    violence or abuse.

    …

[40] In its judgment or reasons the court should always make
clear how its findings on the issue of domestic violence or
abuse have influenced its decision on the issue of
arrangements for the child. In particular, where the court has
found domestic violence or abuse proved but nonetheless
makes an order which results in the child having future
contact with the perpetrator of domestic violence or abuse,
the court should always explain, whether by way of reference
to the welfare check-list the factors in paragraphs 36 and 37

or otherwise, why it takes the view that the order which it has made is safe and beneficial for the child.

It is of note that from a non-Convention perspective, the English court may at times be aided by bilateral treaty agreement such as that which operates between the judiciary in the UK and Pakistan on child abduction, named the *UK-Pakistan Protocol (2003)*, which has existed for 20 years. To this effect, the English court may make orders referring to the Protocol (it is not law), and judges in Pakistan are able to bear the Protocol in mind (with a somewhat mirror habeas corpus approach) (see PD12F part 6).

Tipstaff

Orders made in the High Court may be enforced with the support of Tipstaff, the enforcement office for all High Court Orders. Application orders such as a passport seizure order, if it is intended to be held by Tipstaff (rather than a neutral party, e.g., a firm of solicitors), would need to be addressed to Tipstaff. The role of Tipstaff in child abduction cases typically involve locating children, taking them into protective custody and actioning the seizure of travel documents (see PD12D para.7.1).

Passport order

An order requiring the taking parent to surrender any passports or travel documents (usually relating to the child only) to deter any further removal out of the jurisdiction (e.g., re-abduction) while proceedings are ongoing.

Port Alert

The making of a Port Alert Order will seek to prevent the removal of the child from the jurisdiction, with police assistance, by a warning to all ports in the UK and out of the country who will hold the name of the child at risk of any further unlawful removal in the context of an ongoing child abduction case. See for example, *A v B (Port Alert)* [2021] EWHC 1716 (Fam).

Prohibited Steps Order

A court makes an order prohibiting or restricting the removal of a child from the UK at the risk of e.g., a re-abduction, while proceedings are underway. A Passport Order will be made alongside a Prohibited Steps Order.

Location Order

The making of a Location Order will allow the court to locate the whereabouts of the child in this jurisdiction with the assistance of the Tipstaff.

Collection Order

This order will enable Tipstaff to attend the property where the child is known to be present, to collect the child and place him or her in the care of another, this may also include placement in local authority care.

In addition to the above, for preventative measures prior to international child abduction taking place, practitioners will heed relevant steps such as obtaining a prohibited steps order; gaining a parental responsibility order or obtaining a child arrangements order.

CHAPTER SEVEN

ALTERNATIVE DISPUTE RESOLUTION

7.1 Mediation

Mediation in international parental child abduction cases is voluntary and without prejudice to the parties' right to seek the court's adjudication on contentious matters in the proceedings.

The Family Procedure Rules 2010, Part 3, contains provisions dealing with non-court dispute resolution and the court's duty and power in respect of the same. As per Rule 3.2, these include a duty of the court 'to encourage and facilitate the use of non-court dispute resolution'. Echoing the 1980 Hague Convention itself, Article 7 (c) notes the possibility of securing 'the voluntary return of the child or to bring about an amicable resolution of the issues'. Article 10 reiterates that appropriate measures shall be taken by the Central Authority in the *requested State* to obtain the voluntary return of the child. The Child Abduction Mediation Scheme allows for an independent service, assisted by Reunite, to mediate international child abduction cases. Under the Child Abduction Mediation Scheme, parties are encouraged to speak to a mediator as early as the first on notice hearing, wherein the parties' suitability for mediation is considered during a screening interview. In cases where there are allegations or risk of domestic abuse, the court would have to pay close attention to the appropriateness of encouraging mediation, considering whether it is not only suitable, but also safe. Of note, mediation starts within return proceedings, may run in tandem with proceedings, but the process will not invoke the Article 13(1)(a) exception of acquiescence as per *Re H (Minors) (Abduction: Acquiescence)* [1998] AC [88]-[89]. To summarise, the President's Practice Guidance on Case Management and Mediation provides that:

3.3. The Child Abduction Mediation Scheme will operate in parallel with, but independent from, the proceedings. Where parties agree to enter into mediation, the court will give any directions required to facilitate the mediation. The parties or the parties' representatives must be in a position to address the court on the question of mediation at the relevant hearing to enable the court to consider the appropriateness of such directions. The mediation will proceed with the aim of completing that mediation within the applicable timescales. Where the mediation is successful, the resulting Memorandum of Understanding will be drawn up into a consent order for approval by the court. If the mediation is not successful, the court will proceed to determine the application.

7.2 Family Agreements Practitioners Tool

As part of a shift towards greater use of alternative methods of dispute resolution, the recently published HCCH *Practitioners' Tool: Cross-Border Recognition and Enforcement of Agreements Reached in the Course of Family Matters Involving Children*[161] hopes to increase non-court procedures to bring about autonomous agreed solutions between parties. In essence, mediated agreements that can be endorsed by the court and therefore recognised and enforced in another jurisdiction. Whereas the Experts' Group on Cross Border Recognition and Enforcement of Agreements in International Child Disputes was tasked with considering all possible solutions including the desirability of an instrument, a comprehensive Practitioners Tool was endorsed.

Family agreement is an agreement in the area of family law involving children and a subject matter that falls within the scope of the 1980 Hague Convention, 1996 Hague Convention and / or the 2007 Hague

---

[161] https://assets.hcch.net/docs/333f37cc-28c9-4b6a-864a-8c335101592c.pdf, accessed on 1 June 2023.

Child Support Convention and includes an agreement between holders of 'parental responsibility'. The Tool only applies where the countries concerned are Contracting States to one or more of the HCCH Conventions, that the Convention in question is in force between the two States and that the family agreement is reached within the framework of the aforementioned Convention(s). Identifying the Convention relevant to the particular situation will depend on the subject matter. In addition, issues relating to 'general private international law rules, substantive family law, or domestic procedural law' do not fall within the scope of the Practitioners' Tool.

During the course of proceedings under the 1980 Hague Convention, parties may reach an agreement by consent. Note that Article 7(c) anticipates agreements on issues that may not necessarily be a return order. Notably, the Tool encourages all types of voluntary agreements, not just mediation. This may include one or a combination of the following outcomes: a return agreement, a non-return agreement, agreement on cross border relocation and/or agreement on cross border contact. The Family Agreements Practitioners Tool also explores, amongst others, issues arising such as best interest considerations, the concept of 'habitual residence' and legal validity and enforceability, and practitioners are encouraged to appraise themselves of its content. To summarise, the Tool observes that a child may be heard through a variety of means apart from their direct participation in the proceedings for a measure of protection incorporating the family agreement.[162] The weight to be given to an agreement on habitual residence will depend on the overall circumstances of the case;[163] and it is important to distinguish legal validity and enforceability. An agreement will only have practical effect if it is legally valid. An agreement (or parts of it) might have

---

[162] HCCH Practitioners' Tool: Cross-Border Recognition and Enforcement of Agreements Reached in the Course of Family Matters Involving Children, para. 65.

[163] ibid, para. 67.

immediate legal validity, but for enforceability a further step may be required.[164]

---

[164] ibid, para. 69.

CHAPTER EIGHT

TRANS-FRONTIER CONTACT

One of the 1980 Hague Conventions objectives as per Article 1(b) is 'to ensure that rights of custody and of access under the law of one Contracting State are effectively respected in the other Contracting States.' Thus, under the 1980 Hague Convention, parents may seek to secure rights of access, in other words 'contact' or 'spend time with' child arrangements, pursuant to Article 21 of the Convention. However, although it is an objective of the 1980 Hague Convention to 'secure protection for rights of access', provisions within the Convention on this matter are limited. Even so, legal co-operation to support contact rights, whether to make or modify decisions by other member States, gives the 1980 Hague Convention clout in this arena.

Article 21 provides that:

> An application to make arrangements for organising or securing the effective exercise of rights of access may be presented to the Central Authorities of the Contracting States in the same way as an application for the return of a child.

> The Central Authorities are bound by the obligations of co-operation which are set forth in Article 7 to promote the peaceful enjoyment of access rights and the fulfilment of any conditions to which the exercise of those rights may be subject. The Central Authorities shall take steps to remove, as far as possible, all obstacles to the exercise of such rights.

> The Central Authorities, either directly or through intermediaries, may initiate or assist in the institution of proceedings with a view to organising or protecting these rights and securing respect for the conditions to which the exercise of these rights may be subject.

This provision is supported by the HCCH Guide to Good Practice on Transfrontier Contact Concerning Children.[165] As per the Guide, for the purposes of Article 21, rights of custody is regarded as rights of access/contact.[166] Practitioners should be aware that Article 21 instructions to pursue effective rights of access may arise from a variety of circumstances, whether as a standalone application or in the context of an abduction where an application for the return of a child is withdrawn or unsuccessful. Notably this also includes circumstances where a relative or other non-parent without custody rights (or in other words, holders of parental responsibility) are seeking contact pursuant to Article 21. See generally preceding chapters on establishing custody rights including inchoate rights of custody. As in the case of *A & B v C (Hague Convention: Rights of Access)*[167] which concerned the applicant grandmother and aunt, it is possible for a non-parent without custody rights to rely on Article 12 of the Convention.

Professor Pérez-Vera makes it clear that the Article as a whole rests on co-operation among Central Authorities, who are tasked with organising, securing, or promoting access rights by initiating or facilitating judicial or administrative proceedings, whether directly or through intermediaries. Remembering that private international law, such as the 1980 Hague Convention seeks to harmonise substantive domestic laws, Article 21 is essentially the pathway to provisions under the 1989

---

[165] HCCH, Guide to Good Practice on Trans-frontier Contact Concerning Children, 2008 (hereafter 'Guide to Good Practice on Transfrontier Contact').

[166] ibid, p.xix.

[167] [2018] EWHC 2048 (Fam), [2019] 1 FLR 429.

Children Act. Article 21 of its own volition does not confer a jurisdiction for the English court to determine matters of access or recognition or enforcement of access orders (see *Re G (A Minor) (Hague Convention: Access)* [1993] 1 FLR 669). No doubt the circumstances of each individual case would determine the extent to which Article 21 may apply. However, 'the right to apply under Article 21 of the 1980 Hague Convention to make arrangements for recognising or securing the effective exercise of 'rights of access' should not be limited to cases where there is an existing court order recognition or establishing rights of access, but should include cases where the applicant relies on access rights which arise by operation of law or has status to seek the establishment of such rights'.[168] Nevertheless, where jurisdiction is concerned, common jurisdictional standards dictate that courts should ensure that they have the right to make decisions concerning contact in the interests of the child. The obvious would-be jurisdiction on the basis of habitual residence. In the realm of cross-border contact cases conflict of laws may arise as to the recognition and enforceability of orders made in one jurisdiction. So, for example, the case of *Re G (A Minor) (Hague Convention: Access)* [1993] 1 FLR 669,[169] involved the English and Canadian (Ontario) court which commenced in 1990 with the mother's wrongful removal of the child to England. Initially, the abduction led to a return order to Canada. In 1991, the mother subsequently obtained leave to permanently remove the child from the jurisdiction back to England, by virtue of a consent order for custody to the mother with access rights (contact) to the father. That order granted contact in Ontario, but the mother refused to comply with it. Pursuant to an application under Articles 7 and 21 of the 1980 Hague Convention, the father sought the implementation of the Ontario consent court order as it stood. At first instance, taking into account the welfare of the child, Cazalet J made orders granting contact in Ontario in a gradual and

---

[168] Guide to Good Practice on Trans-frontier Contact, p.xix.

[169] Also known as Re G. (A Minor) (Enforcement of Access Abroad) [1993] Fam 216, [1993] 2 WLR 825. See subsequently *H v M* [2005] EWCA Civ 976, [2005] 2 FLR 1119.

progressive way by directing the first two in England in the summer and Christmas of 1992 before contact in Canada in the summer of 1993. On appeal, the Court of Appeal rejected the argument that 'the state of habitual residence would continue to govern the affairs and welfare of a child living permanently elsewhere'. In essence, the child, though habitually resident in Ontario at the time the Ontario consent order was made, had become habitually resident in England by the time the mother refused to comply with the order. Although Article 21 did apply to the father's claim for effective exercise of rights of custody, it was correctly decided by the trial judge to revert to determining the application under the legal framework of national law,[170] that being the key principles under the Children Act 1989 including the welfare of the child being the paramount consideration. All the while recognising the Canadian order as an 'important part of the history of the child'.[171] As a result, one would expect the usual approach to include any considerations under PD12J and the requirement for a Cafcass' welfare report.

Article 7(f) reminds Central Authorities to co-operate with each other and to promote such co-operation in achieving the Convention's other objectives including 'to initiate or facilitate the institution of judicial or administrative proceedings with a view to obtaining the return of the child and, in a proper case, to make arrangements for organising or securing the effective exercise of rights of access.' Practitioners should at the earliest stage of any such application consider the nature and suitability of the contact pursued, especially in a cross-border context. Having said that, the inter-jurisdictional dynamics should not deter practitioners from reflecting on the rights of the child, to preserve his or her identify and, in the absence of any safeguarding issues, to maintain contact with their parents even if they live in different countries.

---

[170] Of course, a similar issue today would be addressed by engaging the 1996 Hague Convention.

[171] ibid.

CHAPTER NINE

SOME CURRENT ISSUES

9.1 Child Participation

Children, as 'moral actors in their own right' should be afforded the opportunity to properly and fully participate in proceedings. A child is just as key a protagonist in Hague cases as any parent, and thus practitioners on either side should be alert to the issue of child participation. In the context of Article 13(2) in particular, English jurisprudence is ample but as research builds on the current state, there is room for improvement. Professor Rhona Schuz makes the point that child participation is not only instrumental but has independent value.[172] Professors Freeman and Taylor further reiterate that with the court decision being a 'defining moment in a child's life',[173] and thus the opportunity for a child to use their own voice including directly to a judge, should be welcomed. In the case of *C v B* [2019] EWHC 2593 (Fam) the judge met all three children in the presence of the CAFCASS Officer and a note taker, taking into account the Guidance for Judges Meeting Children who are subject to Family Proceedings (April 2010). Though few and far in between, recalling even the observations of

---

[172] Rhona Schuz, 'Child Participation and the Child Objection Exception', in M Freeman and Nicola Taylor (ed.), *Research Handbook on International Child* Abduction (Edward Elgar 2023) 115-130.

[173] Marilyn Freeman and Nicola Taylor, 'Domestic violence and child participation: contemporary challenges for the 1980 Hague child abduction convention', *Journal of Social Welfare and Family Law*, (2020) 42:2, p.167. See also generally, Freeman M, 'The Child Perspective in the context of the 1980 Hague Convention' (October 2020), EU Policy Department for Citizens' Rights and Constitutional Affairs.

Thorpe LJ in *Re G (Children)* [2010] EWCA Civ 1232 (albeit unusual at Court of Appeal level) it is feasible. As articulated by Fenton Glynn, 'the child should be the subject of the proceedings, not the object'.[174] The hearing of a child is a fundamental principle under the UNCRC. It is a principle that is of 'universal application' and 'consistent with…international obligations' under the UNCRC. Article 12 (2) of the UNCRC provides the fundamental principle that '…the child shall in particular be provided the opportunity to be heard in any judicial and administrative proceedings affecting the child, either directly, or through a representative or an appropriate body, in a manner consistent with the procedural rules of national law'. Article 24 of the EU Charter of Fundamental Rights also reiterates that children have the right to 'express their view freely. Such views shall be taken into consideration on matters which concern them in accordance with their age and maturity'.

9.2 Migrant Parents

One of the unintended consequences of the implementation of the 1980 Hague Convention is the impact of the Convention on children and their migrant mothers, especially where reliance is placed on the Article13(1)*b)* grave risk of harm. It creates socio-legal contexts that is not devoid of its challenges. This is on the background of a return to the child's country of habitual residence, a country that the respondent parent may view themselves as an immigrant. There are socio-economic characteristics from precarious immigration status to labour market positions to isolation[175] and mental health difficulties that foster a distinct level of

---

[174] C Fenton-Glynn, 'Participation and Natural Justice: Children's Rights and Interests in Hague Abduction Proceedings', (2014) 9 J. Comp.L, 144. See also Carolyn Hamilton, 'Children's Rights and the role of the UN Committee on the Rights of the Child: Underlying structures for States in implementing the Convention on the Rights of the Child' (2010) International Family Law 31-50.

[175] The GlobalArrk charity refers to the term 'stuck' parents. A 'stuck parent' is a parent who is unable to lawfully return to live in the country they

vulnerability. Whilst a defence may be pursued under the Article 13(1)*b)* exception, such as mounting an argument of material disadvantage and financial hardship for example, it has so far been less than persuasive in the English Court. The impact that flows from situation on primary carer migrant mothers on their children is deserving of attention.

9.3 The Grave Risk of Harm

The Guide to Good Practice on Article 13(1)*b)* was as a direct response to the inconsistencies in the interpretation and application of the grave risk of harm exception. These inconsistencies can be seen not only across jurisdictions but within them (see for example UK POAM National Report[176]). The main shift that can be seen is the clarification in the Guide post the *Re E* and *Re S* era that subsequent case law has sought to address; namely the approach to allegations of domestic abuse under Article 13(1)*b)* – does one assume the risk at its highest or conduct an evaluative exercise. The Guide to Good Practice on Article 13(1)*b)* is about 3 years old and it would be interesting to reflect on its influence and impact on the quest for uniformity.

---

consider 'home' with their children after an international residence/ custody dispute. Stuck parents often struggle with issues such as loneliness, unemployment, language barriers, visa restrictions and lack of legal status (GlobalARRK website, 2022). GlobalARRK is a charity that supports parents and children involved in the child abduction and relocation proceedings, https://www.globalarrk.org/.

[176] K Trimmings, O Momoh, I Callander 'Protection of Abducting Mothers in Return Proceedings: Intersection between Domestic Violence and Parental Child Abduction: UK National Report' (2019) EU funded report. This report was funded by the European Union's Rights, Equality and Citizenship Programme (2014-2020). https://research.abdn.ac.uk/wp-content/uploads/sites/15/2020/02/National-report_UK.pdf, accessed 1 June 2023.

9.4 Fair Representation (Access to Legal Aid)

The provision of legal aid is a vital part of access to justice. In 1980 Hague Convention proceedings, respondent parents are at an immediate disadvantage because they are not eligible for legal aid unless they pass a means and merit test. Whereas the applicant (left behind) parent receives free and automatic legal aid from advice to mediation to representation at court. When the respondent is not on equal footing, this can result in being at a disadvantage from the outset: a delay in legal advice' difficulties with un-translated documents, limited or no access to interpreters outside the court proceedings themselves, obtaining inadequate legal advice from non-expert practitioners with subsequent impact on the quality and standard of pleadings and appearing as a litigant in person in the High Court due to financial constraints. Without adequate legal representation, arguably the right to a fair hearing is threatened, especially for often vulnerable respondents seeking to rely on exceptions to return such as Article 13(1)*b)*, Article 20 and Article 13(2).

It can be argued that the provision of legal aid for both sides is integral to access to justice; it could be that for a respondent it is merits but not means tested. Article 6 of the 1998 Human Rights Act 1 reflects on the right to a fair hearing: 'in the determination of his civil rights and obligations or of any criminal charge against him, everyone is entitled to a fair and public hearing within a reasonable time by an independent and impartial tribunal established by law...'. In 2019, the Ministry of Justice released an action plan entitled '*Legal Support: The Way Ahead: An action plan to deliver better support to people experiencing legal problems*', *Ministry of Justice* (2019).[177] Part of the MoJ's proposals for reform in relation to Legal Aid included 'improving access for vulnerable groups' such as separated children in immigration cases. The intersectionality between immigration and the cross-border movement of children is surely

---

https://assets.publishing.service.gov.uk/government/uploads/system/upload s/attachment_data/file/777036/legal-support-the-way-ahead.pdf, accessed 1 June 2023.

persuasive, not lest due to the vulnerability of taking parents who are fleeing from domestic abuse.

CHAPTER TEN

CONCLUDING REMARKS

In England and Wales, international parental child abduction is tackled via two very contrasting approaches, despite common objectives to protect children from the harmful effects of child abduction. Whereas the 1980 Hague Convention is driven by the restoration of the *status quo ante* and thus invoking the summary return mechanism; under the inherent jurisdiction of the High Court, it is effectively a welfare exercise. The impact of international parental child abduction on a child does not discriminate between Convention and non-Convention situations, and yet it ought to be observed that very different outcomes may ensue depending on the interacting country. Perhaps this is motivation after all for non-Convention countries to ratify or accede to the 1980 Hague Convention.

The very complex prism of an ever-evolving landscape of national and international instruments (especially since Brexit) has influenced our common law jurisprudence. Indeed, English case law in the field of parental child abduction is deserving of acknowledgement, with judicial decisions and case management processes that have reacted to societal and legal changes, especially since the inception of the 1980 Hague Convention. Recalling the introductory observations to this book, child abduction is a specialist branch of family law and those we represent are deserving of that competency. In the same way that the concentration of jurisdiction is one of the bedrocks of our courts' procedural flair; whilst the same cannot be said about whose doors or pigeonhole child abduction cases may land, especially when dealing with a respondent defending a return application, it is hoped that this book will bridge the gap and give practitioners the skill base to act immediately and effectively.

MORE BOOKS BY
LAW BRIEF PUBLISHING

A selection of our other titles available now:-

'A Practical Guide to Estate Administration and Crypto Assets' by Richard Marshall
'A Practical Guide to Managing GDPR Data Subject Access Requests – Second Edition' by Patrick O'Kane
'A Practical Guide to Parental Alienation in Private and Public Law Children Cases' by Sam King QC & Frankie Shama
'Contested Heritage – Removing Art from Land and Historic Buildings' by Richard Harwood QC, Catherine Dobson, David Sawtell
'The Limits of Separate Legal Personality: When Those Running a Company Can Be Held Personally Liable for Losses Caused to Third Parties Outside of the Company' by Dr Mike Wilkinson
'A Practical Guide to Transgender Law' by Robin Moira White & Nicola Newbegin
'Artificial Intelligence – The Practical Legal Issues (2nd Edition)' by John Buyers
'A Practical Guide to Residential Freehold Conveyancing' by Lorraine Richardson
'A Practical Guide to Pensions on Divorce for Lawyers' by Bryan Scant
'A Practical Guide to Challenging Sham Marriage Allegations in Immigration Law' by Priya Solanki
'A Practical Guide to Legal Rights in Scotland' by Sarah-Jane Macdonald
'A Practical Guide to New Build Conveyancing' by Paul Sams & Rebecca East
'A Practical Guide to Defending Barristers in Disciplinary Cases' by Marc Beaumont
'A Practical Guide to Inherited Wealth on Divorce' by Hayley Trim
'A Practical Guide to Practice Direction 12J and Domestic Abuse in Private Law Children Proceedings' by Rebecca Cross & Malvika Jaganmohan
'A Practical Guide to Confiscation and Restraint' by Narita Bahra QC, John Carl Townsend, David Winch
'A Practical Guide to the Law of Forests in Scotland' by Philip Buchan
'A Practical Guide to Health and Medical Cases in Immigration Law' by Rebecca Chapman & Miranda Butler

These books and more are available to order online direct from the publisher at www.lawbriefpublishing.com, where you can also read free sample chapters. For any queries, contact us on 0844 587 2383 or mail@lawbriefpublishing.com.

Our books are also usually in stock at www.amazon.co.uk with free next day delivery for Prime members, and at good legal bookshops such as Wildy & Sons.

We are regularly launching new books in our series of practical day-to-day practitioners' guides. Visit our website and join our free newsletter to be kept informed and to receive special offers, free chapters, etc.

You can also follow us on Twitter at www.twitter.com/lawbriefpub.